CROSSCURRENTS *Modern Critiques*

CROSSCURRENTS *Modern Critiques*
Harry T. Moore, *General Editor*

Robert Hogan

THE INDEPENDENCE OF
Elmer Rice

WITH A PREFACE BY

Harry T. Moore

Carbondale and Edwardsville

SOUTHERN ILLINOIS UNIVERSITY PRESS

PREFACE

ELMER RICE has had a long, intermittently successful, highly controversial, and often distinguished career in the American theater. He has been energetically versatile: to name three of his plays which have caught on, there are the breathlessly melodramatic On Trial, the daringly expressionistic The Adding Machine, and the brutally realistic Street Scene. Altogether, as Rice has said, he has written "some fifty full-length plays (about twenty of them unproduced)," as well as several novels and hundreds of articles. Fortunately, in the present book Robert Hogan—who teaches at the University of California, Davis—isn't bogged down by this mass. He makes his way through it admirably.

That Elmer Rice has inevitably written some trash, Mr. Hogan doesn't hesitate to say. But he does try to find what is good, and particularly what is best, in Rice, and he presents discerning criticism of his discoveries. No one is going to agree with all he says, but at least he doesn't deliver thumping generalities. If he makes a broad statement, he sandbags it with sturdy particulars.

Mr. Hogan, who has also written a book on Shean O'Casey, is a man who works inside his craft. He not only teaches drama, as well as other aspects of literature, but he acts in plays and directs them. It is as a man of the theater that he approaches the subject of this book.

And such a volume is both welcome and necessary. Ordinarily, the Crosscurrents/Modern Critiques series doesn't devote itself to authors generally considered to belong among the merely popular rather than the artistically accepted. But Mr. Hogan finds much in Rice that is artistically creditable. Toward the end of his book he works out a canon of Rice's plays, determining which of them belong in various categories of excellence. Throughout, he wages war against current dramatic criticism, particularly that of the New York journalists who sit in judgment on every new play and can make it or break it by a few taps on the typewriter, in articles written in haste in newspaper offices immediately after the curtain has come down on opening night. Not that Mr. Hogan thinks too highly of weekly reviewing, either, or of the magazines devoted to a long-range consideration of modern drama. To back up this point, he gives some interesting (often amusing) examples and statistics.

He calls his book The Independence of Elmer Rice. This reflects Mr. Hogan's own independent mind—for that is certainly what he has. Even when you disagree with his pronouncements, you nevertheless aren't bored by them. The vigor of his searching intellect will keep the reader awake by the continual challenges it offers.

And Mr. Hogan is a technical critic. We need more of this in literature and the drama. It is a kind of criticism that occurs regularly in relation to painting, sculpture, and music. Criticisms of these media are not devoid of discussions of the conceptual, but those who write regularly on art and music keep in mind the technical qualities that make these arts what they are. In literature, alas, the content of ideas is often so impressive that the commentator forgets the importance of other considerations. But, as I say, Mr. Hogan fortunately doesn't.

As a straight writer for the theater, Elmer Rice has the dramatist's gift of compelling the audience's attention—the very success of so many of his plays demonstrates that. I had long ago forgotten, for example, that Rice wrote It is the Law, a play I saw as a boy. Mr. Hogan just mentions it in passing, obviously not considering it worth discussion; and, under the circumstances, this is proper enough. Yet that play—its idea, its contours, its dramatic (really melodramatic) impact—remains fresh in my memory. I think this is mainly attributable to Rice's audience-holding power. Like his earlier On Trial, It is the Law used flash backs; and it gave its leading man a chance to play three parts, himself and two impersonations of others. Arthur Hohl, a fine actor, took excellent advantage of his opportunities; the silent-screen version he made of It is the Law lacked the force of the play partly because Hollywood usually ruins the dramas it adapts and partly because the film couldn't give the effect of Hohl's astonishing vocal changes. But it was something more than the actor, brilliantly as he rose to the occasion, that has kept this melodrama in my mind as it was played on the stage. It was simply what we call good theater.

This ingredient is of course found in the Rice plays, such as Street Scene, which Mr. Hogan and other critics also find artistically acceptable. As Mr. Hogan points out, Street Scene was eventually made into a successful musical drama, with lyrics by Langston Hughes and a score by Kurt Weill. And the play has taken on a new life—since Mr. Hogan's text was written—by becoming, in its original dramatic form, a raging success in the Soviet Union. Also it has, as Mr. Hogan notes, been a staple of college dramatic troupes, along with other plays by this dramatist; Mr. Hogan provides a table indicating the frequency of recent productions of all of Rice's work.

Another important feature of the present book is its new documentation. Mr. Hogan has had the benefit of a rather copious correspondence with Elmer Rice, from which the playwright has kindly consented to permit lengthy quotations. This helps Mr. Hogan to round out his full picture of Rice's career.

One of the liveliest sections of the volume deals with Mr. Hogan's production of a new Rice play, with the author's help, for a college dramatic society (not at Davis). The inevitable frustrations, the academic bureaucracy, and the campus apathy provide Mr. Hogan with the materials for a good story, of which he makes the most—and it helps to prove many of the points he raises in his valuable, energetic, and thought-provoking book.

HARRY T. MOORE

Southern Illinois University
March 21, 1965

ACKNOWLEDGMENTS

A BOOK IS ALWAYS a collaboration, and my chief collaborators were Joseph Baranowski, Daniel J. Walkowitz, Marc J. Weiss, Hubert La Temple, Daniel Geringer, and the students of my playwriting class at the University of Rochester. My thanks must also go to Professor Sven Eric Molin of Randolph-Macon Women's College for his close and thoughtful perusal of the manuscript, and to the librarians at the University of Rochester who afforded me every convenience.

My chief thanks, of course, must go to Elmer Rice for his encouragement, advice, criticism, and hospitality, for allowing me to produce *Love among the Ruins*, and for sitting in on rehearsals long enough to ensure that it could not be called *Love among the Mess*. Whatever insight this book contains is largely a paraphrase of what I have found in Rice's own writings; the foolishness here is original.

ROBERT HOGAN

Davis, California
November, 1964

CONTENTS

THE INDEPENDENCE OF
Elmer Rice

THE LAST QUARTER of the nineteenth century saw the triumph of Ibsen and the spread of the new drama through Europe, but that new drama made little initial impression in America. Until after the First World War, American drama remained devoted to the pseudo-realistic entertainments of David Belasco and to the melodramatic spectacles developed by Dion Boucicault and others in the nineteenth century. The American stage was enveloped in a fog of melodrama, murder, low comedy, and stock patriotism. Two aphorisms of George M. Cohan, which Elmer Rice is fond of quoting, are fair indications of theatrical taste of the time: "Always leave them laughing when you say good-bye," and "The American flag has saved many a bum show."

Clyde Fitch's posthumous play, *The City*, produced in 1910, did contain the startling words, "God damn," and was an honest attempt to grapple with the realities of American life. Fitch, however, was the best product of an earlier age, and *The City*, when compared to plays like *Ghosts* or *Mrs. Warren's Profession* by his European contemporaries Ibsen and Shaw, seems timid and awkward. The prominent American critic William Winter could, as late as 1913, write of Ibsen:

> A reformer who calls you to crawl with him into a sewer merely to see and breath its feculence is a pest. . . . Ibsen's dramas, when treating of the relations of sex— notably in *Hedda Gabler*, *Rosmersholm* and *Ghosts*—

treat them as affected under the reaction of disease, and thus they fill the mind, whether of the reader or the auditor, with disgust and gloom: they pervert life: they tend to disseminate misinformation, augment ignorance, and mislead weak or ill-educated minds, and therein they are immoral. . . . Ibsen, as a writer of variously flaccid, insipid, tainted, obfuscated, and nauseous plays, could be borne, although, even in that aspect, he is an offence to taste and a burden on the patience, but Ibsen obtruded as a sound leader of thought is a grotesque absurdity. . . . The explanation of Ibsen . . . is, unquestionably, a disordered brain.

On October 31, 1905, the *New York Herald* reviewed Arnold Daly's production of *Mrs. Warren's Profession* by saying, "The only way successfully to expurgate *Mrs. Warren's Profession* is to cut the whole play out. You cannot have a clean pig stye." The *Sun* called the play "a dramatized stench." The *Evening Post* said it was "at once contemptible and abominable." The *Times* concluded that, "Mr. Shaw takes a subject, decaying and reeking, and analyzes it for the edification of those whose unhealthy tastes find satisfaction in morbific suggestion."

Such was the state of the New York stage in the first decade or two of this century.

If one had to draw a dividing line between the modern drama and the old in America, the year 1914 would not be a bad choice. That year saw the beginnings of a conflict which would draw the United States forever from its cocoon of parochialism, and that year in the theatre saw the first hints of the modern American drama. A young man, Eugene G. O'Neill, the son of a famous actor-manager of the old school, published his first one-act plays in a slim volume titled *Thirst*. Another young man, Elmer L. Reizenstein, had his first play *On Trial* produced on Broadway. *Thirst* went unnoticed, but *On Trial* was hugely successful. It ran for 365 performances in New York; three touring companies played it in such (to modern ears) surprising places as Eau Claire, Mankato, Waco, Hot Springs, and Altoona; it spawned dozens of imitations; it became a film and a novel; it was produced in

Argentina, Australia, Austria, Canada, France, Germany, Holland, Hungary, Ireland, Japan, Mexico, Norway, Scotland, and South Africa; and it earned its twenty-one-year-old author the still dazzling figure of $100,000.

These two young men, O'Neill and Reizenstein—or, as we now know him, Rice—were the first American dramatists whom we could call either modern or excellent. However, in their wake, in the 1920's, came Maxwell Anderson, Philip Barry, S. N. Behrman, Paul Green, Sidney Howard, George Kelly, Edwin Justus Mayer, and Robert E. Sherwood. With this array of talent, the American drama was firmly established as one of the exciting and vital theatres of the world.

In recent years, most of these playwrights have either died or retired. O'Neill is still very much a part of the contemporary theatre, but largely because his superb posthumous plays saved him from the neglect into which he began to fall immediately after his death. Rice had a play in New York in 1958 and Behrman in 1963, but for the most part these early practitioners of our modern drama have been superseded—first by Odets and Saroyan, then by Williams, Miller, and Inge, and now by Albee, Kopit, and Richardson. The new dramatists are no better than the old, but the theatre, as Rice once remarked, is treated in this country as news and not as art.

This situation has been accepted without demur by college and community theatres which are more interested in today's Broadway success than in yesterday's masterpiece. Even the professors who anthologize plays and who should remind us of the excellences of the past largely follow the lead of the dramatic journalists, and puff those writers currently successful. University students tend to know the work of Williams, Miller, and Albee, but only the best informed have heard of Rice, Anderson, or Sherwood.

American poets and novelists have received more than their share of attention from scholars and critics, but American playwrights have remained largely untouched either by the new critical methods or by the traditional approaches of the scholar. So, while American poets and novelists of the past are continually reinterpreted to today's audience, American playwrights, even of as recent a past as the 1920's, remain dimly remembered names.

This situation is unhealthy, for a living literature is permeated by a sense of the accomplishment of the past, and the excellence of Williams and Miller rests more than we nowadays allow upon the excellence of their predecessors. The dramatists of the 1920's and '30's are important even beyond their having created a theatre in which the plays of Williams and Miller could be produced. They are important because their best work retains an enduring vitality. There are many half-forgotten plays that belong in the continuing repertoire of the American theatre and in the living consciousness of playwrights and playgoers, if the American theatre is to retain its freshness, its direction, and its life.

ii

The American theatre is an economic institution, a business, a commercial enterprise. This commercial basis has been in many ways healthy. It has created around our theatre an aura of riches, richness, and glamor, and that theatre has produced since 1914 a roster of distinguished plays and playwrights. It has reinvigorated at least one dramatic genre, the musical comedy. It has changed in the last half century the theatrical habits of the nation and to some measurable extent of the world.

Despite such credits, the commercial theatre has probably repressed the drama more than fostered it. When its plays are chosen for probable commercial success, it would seem improbable that the best plays are always chosen. When the only qualification needed to become a commercial producer is enough money to produce a play, it would seem improbable that the taste of every producer is impeccable. There are superb plays that go abegging for a production, that become ever more dog-eared as they are shuffled more or less unread from one producer's desk to another, and that finally die in some lost limbo of forgotten manuscripts.

In *The Fervent Years,* for example, Harold Clurman describes how the Group Theatre failed to raise enough money to produce Padraic Colum's *Balloon.* Some thirty years later, Mr. Colum, still peddling the script, sent it to me, rather ruefully calling it "the most famous unproduced play on Broadway." In my own short and scrappy career on various amateur stages, I have produced or directed premières of three interesting plays by O'Casey, one by Paul Vincent Carroll, and one by Rice. Had the opportunity been present, I could have staged several times that number of plays by established writers, as well as some meritorious new scripts by unknown writers. I am convinced that the modern drama is greater in both quantity and quality than the commercial stage has allowed us to discover. I am convinced that we have a large, lost repertoire of plays that will never find the boards so long as we depend upon the commercial producer to form our taste.

A second unhealthy quality of the commercial stage is the long run. The main interest of producers is a return on their money, and so they are interested in milking all commercial value from a play. The longer the run, the better for the producer's purse. The effect of the long run is both good and bad. It is a boon for actors and technicians, but it also fosters a false evaluation of plays. It helps to create shoddy taste and poor standards because negligible plays sometimes are popular and fine plays sometimes fail. The commercial failure is almost always doomed to oblivion, no matter what its merits, and this hit-and-miss kind of evaluation determines the modern repertoire.

Many matters unconnected with artistic merit can make a play succeed or fail on Broadway. A play depends upon dozens of people—carpenters, electricians, and ushers as well as actors, producers, and directors. Any of these myriad folk might botch a show, and so also might events totally outside the theatre. The headlines of the newspaper and the fluctuations of the weather may have as strong an effect as the vagaries of a star or the eccentricities of a reviewer. Often commercial success or failure baffles analysis, and a play that succeeded in New York or London often fails when transported across the Atlantic. Rice's *Judgment Day* was contemptuously dismissed in the United States and yet was later hailed as one of the best plays of the London season. These facts and many others make it impossible to accept commercial success as any highly valid index of merit.

A third unhealthy effect of the commercial theatre is the premium placed upon newness and originality. Today's dramatist is often puffed beyond his merits, while the dramatist of yesterday, no matter how worthy his play, is largely ignored. Brilliance does not appear every season, but there would be fewer plaints about the decline of the drama if our current plays were mounted alongside the best plays of our recent past. We would then have a salient reminder of high standards, and it would be difficult for reviewers to fall into such fulsome adulation as, "Best damn play I've seen for years."

These dangers of the commercial stage should be combated by the community or at least by the campus theatres, but unfortunately both largely follow the lead of Broadway. If one scans the lists of plays to be found in *Theatre Arts* or *Players' Magazine,* one discovers a depressing monotony of choice in the selections of campus and community theatres. The same plays are presented everywhere simultaneously, and the plays presented are those that two years previously were the smash hits of Broadway or the West End. Even the so-called "experimental" theatres imitatively present the same experiments. A few years ago the favorite authors were Genêt and Ionesco, and then Pinter and Albee, and now Max Frisch and Arthur Kopit. The amateur theatres seem to be moving together in robotlike lockstep.

There is some excuse for the lightweight repertoire of the community theatre whose people are more interested in recreation than in art, but there seems little excuse for the college theatre. There one should see the classic American plays periodically revived and the doors invitingly opened to young dramatists. Most college theatres, however, presented a depressingly "well-rounded" program, which is calculated to woo first of all a lowbrow audience, and only secondarily to fulfil the minimum demands of "culture." That program consists first of the Traditional Classic—most frequently a Shakespeare, adorned by the costumes of 1600 and the staging of 1920. Second, it contains a Modern Classic—almost inevitably Ibsen, Chekhov, Strindberg, or Shaw. If the college is undistinguished, the program is likely to contain a musical or light comedy. If the college has some intellectual pretensions, the program would probably contain an example or two of whatever is currently admired by *Time* magazine—nowadays, Tennessee Williams.

At present, American drama is originated on Broadway, that thoroughfare which Rice once called "the tawdriest street in the world." The flow of plays is all one way, from Broadway to the provinces. Until the commercial theatre destroys itself by high costs and the abject prostitution of value, we can count on little of greatness emerging from it, and the only hope seems to be for some reversal of the flow. The amateur stage itself must begin to add to the stock of the living theatre, for until the flow of plays rises from the whole country we will never realize the dramatic greatness that we inherently possess.

iii

One reason for the neglect of Rice and for the weakened condition of the stage has been the lack of an intelligent criticism. No startling manifesto is intended by that statement; it is a truism that has been uttered by practically every intelligent writer, actor, director, or producer in the business. This volume makes no claim to remedy that lack; it is only a tentative groping in what seems, to my mind, the proper direction for dramatic criticism to take.

A word seems necessary about that direction. From the welter of conflicting theories of the drama that have been developed from Aristotle to Eric Bentley, little clarity has emerged. Until the late nineteenth century, critics seemed more intent on testing dramatic theories by occasional references to plays, rather than plays by occasional references to theories. The bent was toward aesthetics rather than criticism, and criticism suffered. The few good critics had to spend much of their time defending the masterpieces of Shakespeare from neo-Aristotelians who preferred *Gorboduc* for not violating the three unities.

The critics who followed that magnificent exception to rules, Bernard Shaw, were less concerned with such academic problems. Most of the notable post-Shavian critics have been journalists more trained in reportage than in the history of the drama. The theatrical journalist avoids sterile theorizing and concentrates primarily upon the play, but he has few standards to guide him other than the instinctual cry of the man in the street: "I liked it. I don't know why, but I did." Consequently, the opinions of the journalist-critics wear little better than the opinions of such learned predecessors as Scaliger and Sidney.

If the journalist-critic treats the drama almost exclusively as news, the modern academic critic, as a descendant of Scaliger and Sidney, treats it almost exclusively as literature. The journalist, relying solely upon the emotional effects produced upon him or upon the news value of the play, is content merely to approve or disapprove. The academic, training upon the play the devastating barrage of critical artillery appropriate for the modern poem, often discovers no merit in any play. His approach seems so beside the point that it exerts little effect upon the drama, and is relegated to the pages of a few small circulation magazines read mostly by other academics. The journalistic approach does exert much influence, however, and in those large cities of the world that produce new plays the opinions of a half dozen reviewers can make or break a play. In the opinions of those who should best know—the playwrights, actors, and directors—neither the academic nor the journalistic approach is worth much consideration. Academic criticism is so remote from practical stagecraft that it has nothing to say to the man of the theatre, and the opinions of the journalist are usually considered so ignorant or irresponsible that his praise is often valued less than his condemnation.

A good play may be both literature and news, but it is something more than either, something which has been traditionally described as theatre. To my mind, the appropriate criticism for theatre is found in the reviews of Shaw. Such a rare and superb criticism bases itself upon the performance and not upon the text, but it is also impelled by theory. The theory does not fit plays into Procrustean beds of genre, but arises from the plays themselves and never becomes so sacrosanct that it cannot be modified or even scrapped. It should not be inferred that the theatre has an infallible set of rules or formulas that inevitably produce a succession of hits, or even that the existence of rules and formulas is always conducive to excellence. A staged play is too complicated an organism to ensure frequent success for even the most astute of producers. Yet it is precisely for this reason that the most astute of producers and playwrights have attempted to control as precisely as possible as much as possible.

There is a large body of information handed down in the theatre and modified by each age. This information concerns every facet of production, and the totality of innumerable effects makes a play succeed or fail. A theatrical criticism, then, should be based not merely upon how well Dorine's remark to Tartuffe is phrased in the playscript, but also upon how well she is lighted, made up, costumed, upon her position on the stage, her expression, her tone of voice, upon his expression, his tone of voice, his posture, his reaction, his lighting, make-up and costume, and upon the relation of these matters to what has gone before. Naturally, each minor detail does not require notice in a critique. If it did, the play would be lost in a mass of minutia. Each detail, however, should be in the mind of the critic, and if any detail does not fuse into a meaningful pattern of emotion that grows in a coherent fashion throughout the production, then that detail must be criticized.

Actually, that last remark has a more stuffily "scientific" flavor than I had intended. No criticism can ultimately be reduced to final preciseness. For one thing, a theatrical performance varies each night; sometimes it varies enormously. Yet a theatrical criticism, although it criticizes the play in production, does not criticize the play in a specific performance. One great mistake of the theatrical journalist is in taking the first night's performance as indicative of the real merit of a play; usually a play will not settle down until several performances have passed. A truly theatrical criticism compares the particular performance to the ideal performance. The real merits of any show are based upon this ideal performance which may never be attained, but which the critic can and must infer from what he sees on any specific night. That ideal performance is the show's true value, and a critic must use it as his yardstick.

When one attempts to criticize a body of work like Rice's, the situation is changed again. A theatrical criticism is still necessary, but harder to attain. This book, for instance, evaluates some forty plays, most of which I have never seen and only one of which I know with the thoroughness that comes from having produced it. Still it is necessary to envision from the text of the play the full and ideal performance on the stage. To an extent, such an imagining is beyond the abilities of the most experienced critic. Nevertheless, as theatrical criticism is still criticism, it must make the broader general effort as well as the specific one of the review. If this general effort is not totally successful, it will at least, I believe, be headed in the right direction.

The literary critic who familiarizes himself with Rice's work will be struck by the perspicacity of the author's statements about the drama and the apparently inept execution of some of his work. This conclusion about the awkwardness of the plays is the greatest mistake of the literary approach to the theatre. Usually it results in the patronizing dismissal of plays like—to take an extreme example—*East Lynne*, which has no value as literature. *East Lynne*, if I may speak from my own experience of having directed it and acted the villain's role in it, is even now valid as theatre, and such a realization is probably where a theatrical criticism of the drama must start.

The central conception of Rice's theatre is that the drama is one of the more naïve forms of art, and such a conclusion is inescapable for any dramatist who intends to write more than closet drama. In the Introduction to his volume *Two Plays*, Rice discusses this matter in probing detail, and remarks in part:

> This, then, is the dramatist's real dilemma. Like every other artist, he is interested in projecting reality as he sees it. But he finds himself dependent upon an interpretive medium which is essentially artificial, conservative and conventional. Like every other artist, he wishes, as he matures, to penetrate more and more deeply into his material and to concern himself with inner meanings rather than with external appearances. But he finds himself confronted with an audience, which is untutored, slow of apprehension and impatient of subtleties; an audience, which is eternally on an emotional and intellectual level that can only be described as adolescent.

To this succinct appraisal of the drama's limitations, little need be added. However, if it be asked why an intelligent man should then concern himself with the drama, perhaps only a partially satisfactory answer can be given. If the theatre demands a puerile simplicity, it manages to compensate by investing that simplicity with a greater illusion of reality. Its appeal and its methods are more direct and, in the general sense of the term, dramatic. If the theatre presents a simplified extract from life, that extract may be presented with great impact—indeed, with enough impact to suggest the essence of life. The simplified shortcuts of the stage can move people more strongly, if perhaps less validly, than a novel by, let us say, Henry James.

Theatrical effect is broad and simple, and the theatre demands a basic naïveté from its writers and a suspension of the intellect from its audiences. This is not an unfair demand, for we are repaid ten times over by our strongly evoked emotions. And, indeed, the theatre at its best manages to convince us of its sophistication and profundity. If it is not really sophisticated or profound, neither, it may be argued, is man. At any rate, perhaps enough has been said to suggest that the plays of Rice must not be judged by the rules applied to Dostoevsky's insights into character or James's intricacies of style. If from this discussion, the judicious reader decides that the drama is not for him, he might be reminded that within its narrow limits Sophocles and Shakespeare produced enduring examples of the highest capabilities and aspirations of man. One reason for their monumental excellence is that they were at war with their form. Greatness, it may be argued, in art and in life emerges from such a conflict, such a grinding tension between desire and limitation. Without arguing that Rice is a great playwright, I think it is this same conflict between his aspiration and his form that makes him an interesting one.

RICE HAS BEEN a prolific writer. In his autobiography *Minority Report*, he estimated that he had written:

> some fifty full-length plays (about twenty of them unpro-
> duced); four novels, three of which have been published; a
> book about the theatre; an indeterminate number of short
> stories, one-act plays, articles, book reviews, motion pic-
> tures, radio and television scripts; and the present volume.
> It is an output that falls short of that of Owen Davis, who
> wrote three hundred plays, to say nothing of Lope de Vega,
> who is said to have written eighteen hundred. Still, it is
> substantial.

By my count, Rice has produced or published forty plays, and he specifically refers in his autobiography to thirteen others that were unproduced, unpublished, or unfinished. Of his forty public plays, three are one-acts, four are mime plays, two are adaptations, and five are collaborations. As I write this, he is working on a new play.

This is, as he says, a substantial body of work, but most people interested in the current theatre would be familiar with only a few of the titles—probably *The Adding Machine, Street Scene, Counsellor-at-Law*, and *Dream Girl*. These four, however, neither completely represent Rice at his best, nor completely indicate the different manners in which he has written. Actually, he has worked in a variety of genres. He has essayed with considerable success potboilers, dramas, thesis plays, comedies, fantasies, melodramas, parables, expressionistic fables, and what we might, for lack of a better term, call panoramas. He has written one-acts, mime plays, murder mysteries, and a modern version of *Hamlet*. From this intriguing welter of styles, he once attempted to extract a quality common to all of his work, and it seems appropriate to quote it here.

> What I have been trying to say is simply that there is nothing as important in life as freedom and that the dominant concern not only of every human being, but of all of us as we function as members of society should be with the attainment of freedom of the body and of the mind through liberation from political autocracy, economic slavery, religious superstition, hereditary prejudice and herd psychology and the attainment of freedom of the soul through liberation from fear, jealousy, hatred, possessiveness and self-delusion. Now that I have stated it, I see that I was right in saying that everything I have ever written seriously has had in it no other idea than that.[1]

i

Rice became interested in writing plays when he was a young law clerk and two of his friends asked his opinion about some short plays they had collaborated on. His own first attempt at playwriting, he described in these terms.

> Doubtful of my ability to write a play alone, I persuaded Frank W. Harris to collaborate with me. Of course it had to be a problem play, so we chose as our theme the conflict between a woman's domestic life and her career—a troublesome question even fifty years ago. A small-town wife and mother, outraged by civic corruption, runs for mayor, is elected, but is forced by the deterioration of her marriage to relinquish office. The play was called A *Defection from Grace*, a pun upon the heroine's name, after the manner of *The Importance of Being Earnest*. A prize contest announcement by the Century Theatre Club spurred us on to its completion.[2]

The play won second prize, and Rice and his friend were encouraged to write a second play which they called *The Seventh Commandment*. Of it, Rice remarked:

Again it was a feminist play, this time an attack upon the double standard of morality, the social code that condemns in a woman what it condones in a man. The heroine, trapped in a loveless marriage, leaves her brutish husband for a more compatible mate. Refused a divorce, she chooses to live openly with her lover. But the social pressures are too great; at length they are driven apart. Not long ago I glanced at a surviving copy of this work. The characters are stereotyped and the dialogue is bookish, but the play is moderately well constructed and not altogether unreadable. Nothing ever came of it, though years later the producer Harrison Grey Fiske considered acquiring it as a vehicle for his wife, the celebrated Minnie Maddern Fiske.[3]

The only other apprentice work mentioned in *Minority Report* is a one-act written in 1913 called *The Passing of Chow-Chow*. It won a competition at Columbia University, was produced by the Columbia University Dramatic Association late in 1915, and was published in one of Samuel French's collections of one-act plays in 1925. It is briefly discussed later in this chapter.

With his next attempt, *On Trial*, Rice had the success that every young playwright dreams of. The play was immediately accepted by a sympathetic and intelligent producer, it was produced as quickly as possible, and it was the sensation of the season. Its critical success was as great as its financial success, and the play's reputation lived for years. In 1923, Philip Moeller of the Theatre Guild remarked that, "*On Trial* was something of an event in the American theatre." In 1938, Brooks Atkinson remarked that three of Rice's plays—*On Trial, The Adding Machine*, and *Street Scene*—"have profoundly influenced the technique and thought of the American theatre." And finally the play still gets one or two productions every year.

Rice's own opinion of *On Trial* was less generous but more accurate than that of the critics. He wrote:

> *On Trial* was a shrewd piece of stage carpentry. It was a good show and those who paid to see it got their money's worth. It was nothing more and was never intended to be anything more. I was amazed to find it hailed as a dramatic

masterpiece. Steeped as I was in the theatre of Ibsen and his followers I could not understand how any one could take *On Trial* seriously. It was a salutary awakening for me: it made me realize what the Broadway theatre is like.[4]

Scrutinizing the play today, one finds it difficult to discover what was so impressive. The characters are only theatrical stereotypes; the dialogue is flat and undistinguished. However, the American stage in 1914 was both imitative and lowbrow, and Rice's manner of telling his story was for the times startling and unique. His most usual story is made engrossing by his effective arrangement of the plot, and this feature of the play remains effective still. *On Trial* was not only the first noteworthy experiment of the modern American drama, but also it really was an effective piece of stage carpentry.

Just how much the play was carpentry can be seen by the history of its composition. Rice's central device was suggested by an article of Clayton Hamilton, called "Building a Play Backwards." Here is the most relevant passage.

Might it not be interesting to go a step further and build an entire drama backward—to construct a three-act play, for instance, in which the first act should happen in the autumn, the second act in the preceding summer, and the third act in the previous spring? Let us imagine a tragedy, for instance, in which, with no preliminary exposition, a murder or a suicide is acted out in the initial act. This would naturally awaken in the audience a desire to understand the motives which had culminated in the crime. Then in the second act, we could exhibit the crucial event which had made the murder or the suicide inevitable. Again, the audience would be stimulated to think backward from effects to causes and to wonder what had brought this crucial event about. Lastly in the third act, several previous events could be displayed which would finally clear up the mystery by expounding the initiation of the narrative.[5]

Rice's time sequence covers several years instead of three seasons, but Hamilton's murder plot is basically that of Rice's play. In the first draft of the play, which was called

According to the Evidence, the flashback scenes concerned a Kentucky mountain feud. At the suggestion of
Arthur Hopkins, his producer, Rice scrapped the story of
the feud and substituted the story as it exists today. About
this reworking, Hopkins later wrote:

> Elmer had a splendid idea and a confused story. After I
> bought the play, I told him we would have to begin by
> throwing away the story. He had no objection. Then we
> discussed various stories—finally one definite story began
> to take shape. From that moment, Elmer ground out copy
> like a printing press. Every morning he would come to the
> office with reams of stuff. We would go over it together,
> finally agreeing on which was all right and which was bad.
> In two weeks the play was finished and Elmer had written
> every line, contrary to the belief at the time that I had
> written part of the play.[6]

What Rice retained was his idea of a murder trial which
would act as a framework for the flashback scenes. In one
way, however, the neophyte writer diverged from the
proposal of the professional critic. Rice decided that:

> any play that, so to speak, ended before it began must in-
> evitably be anticlimactic, a difficulty that Hamilton, for
> all his technical knowledge, had ignored. Further examina-
> tion of the formula convinced me that it could be effec-
> tive only if the play *gave the appearance* of moving back-
> ward, while actually it moved forward. For the resolution
> of a situation, which is the essence of drama, must be
> achieved progressively, not retrogressively.[7]

Although Rice's flash backs moved successively farther
back in time, the murder trial, his framework, moved
ahead in the conventional manner of any plot—from, as
Aristotle put it with simple inevitability, beginning to
middle to end. The illustrative flash backs gave the
appearance of moving backward, but they merely clarified
and impelled the forward movement of the true plot, the
murder trial. This structure succeeded in disguising the
triteness of the story and made for an engrossing piece of
theatre. It was a remarkable achievement for a man so
young to handle so excellently such a complicated arrange-

ment, and the play deserved its success. It was good entertainment as well as, for its time, a technical tour de force.

Compared to what his American contemporaries were writing, Rice's dialogue holds up remarkably well. The reason is not vivid writing, but spareness and leanness almost to the point of being skeletal. For instance:

> [TRASK *enters at left.*]
> TRASK Hello, Joan! [MRS. TRASK *turns her back to him and goes down left.*]   Hello, Glover!
> GLOVER Good evening, Mr. Trask.
> [MRS. TRASK *does not answer.*]
> TRASK [*to* MRS. TRASK] What's wrong with you again?
> MRS. TRASK Nothing. [*sits on sofa.*]
> TRASK Oh, is that all?
> GLOVER [*rises*] Allow me—[*he takes hat and coat from* TRASK, *puts them on chair upper right.*]
> TRASK Anything new, Glover?
> GLOVER [*down to table right, where he sits*]   No, sir.
> MRS. TRASK A woman called you up.
> TRASK Oh, that's it. Who was it?
> MRS. TRASK I suppose you know well enough.
> TRASK If I knew I wouldn't ask you. Who was it?
> MRS. TRASK I don't know.

Dialogue like this makes few mistakes. It cannot because it is so spare and tight. It is eminently easy to understand, but not necessarily easy to write. These terse monosyllables must convey a great deal more about their speakers' states of mind than the mere sense content indicates. Still, for all of its stageworthiness, this dialogue is in no way distinguished. It merely carries the play swiftly forward, and puts all of the burden of excellence upon the actor. One drawback of such a style is that it cannot be constantly used; occasionally the writer must try a longer, more emotional flight, and when he does we get something like:

> GLOVER [*springing to his feet*] No, No, Your Honor, it isn't true! I didn't kill him! I took the money, but I didn't kill him! I'll tell you where the money is, I don't

want it. I don't want it! I'll plead guilty—I'll go to jail, but don't arrest me for the murder. I'll tell you how it happened—I'll tell everything. I didn't know Strickland was coming. I planned the robbery that night. When Trask gave me the money I put it in the safe, but I didn't lock the safe. I left it open—he didn't notice it. Then I came back to get the money. I didn't know about Strickland—it's God's truth! Mrs. Trask heard me come in, and I choked her! But she's all right—she's not hurt. That's not murder! I got the money, then I saw Strickland come in. I didn't know he was coming. I didn't. I swear I didn't! I'm innocent! I'm innocent, I tell you!

This will work quite adequately upon the stage, but as characteristic or flavorful or memorable speech it leaves much to be desired.

Rice has grown increasingly fluent as a writer of certain kinds of dialogue. His hand, however, is not consistent, and some of his plays seem written with an excellence curiously lacking in others. Similarly, in later plays, Rice's characterization is sometimes splendidly evocative and sometimes blatantly stereotypical. He seems unsteadier in dialogue and in characterization than in certain other qualities which he has been less often admired for. I have particularly in mind his consistently deft handling of play structure and his continuing experiments in form and in content. These are his consistent excellences, and they appear in his first produced play.

ii

Early in 1917, Hatcher Hughes, with some of his pupils at Columbia University, organized the Morningside Players. This group was typical of a number of amateur organizations of the time, such as The Washington Square Players and the Provincetown Playhouse, and symptomatic of a widespread dissatisfaction with the commercial theatre. The Morningside Players produced two of Rice's plays, the Provincetown Playhouse produced O'Neill, and from The Washington Square Players grew the Theatre

Guild. It seems no exaggeration to say that this little theatre movement was the catalyst which ultimately brought about the dramatic flowering of the 1920's.

The first production of the Morningside Players was Rice's four-act play *The Iron Cross*. The play had earlier been accepted by Arthur Hopkins, but, as he was unable to secure the leading lady he desired, the production did not materialize—a painful, but not unusual experience for a playwright to have on Broadway. The Morningside Players presented the play on February 11 and 13, 1917, at the Comedy Theatre. It was directed by Rice and Will Hutchins. The play has never been revived or published, and Rice recently described it to me as "a museum piece." Still, the playscript reads strongly although its tone is unrelievedly grim. A straightforward indictment of war, its plot has none of the intricacy of *On Trial*, but its dialogue has a bit more body, and the *New York Times* reviewed it well. In a letter Rice described it as "A serious anti-war play, produced on Broadway . . . on the day we broke diplomatic relations with Germany!" In a 1938 article in the *Times*, Rice wrote that it was "probably the first play written about the World War. It was an attempt to debunk the male heroics of militarism in terms of the drama of a soldier's wife whose sole concern is in conserving the enduring emotional value of the home and the family." The wife is a better character than any in *On Trial*, and the theme suggests that Rice, in his serious efforts even at the beginning of his career, was writing plays reflecting the basic issues of the day. He has continued to write such plays, and his *Judgment Day* of 1934, his *American Landscape* of 1938, and his *Flight to the West* of 1940 were among the first plays to call the attention of Americans to a later World War.

The second production of the Morningside Players was on April 22, 1917. It was a bill of four one-acts, which were later published in the booklet *The Morningside Plays*. The last play was *The Home of the Free*, a short, droll comedy of four characters, that satirized enlightened liberalism. Everyone in the Burke household is presumably allowed complete liberty of action and freedom of expression. Consequently, we get such delicious interchanges as this between the father, John Calvin Burke, and his son, Robert Ingersoll Burke.

BURKE   Will you do me the kindness of holding your tongue for a moment? I've a matter of importance to talk to you about.

ROBERT   Don't tell me to hold my tongue! There's nothing of more importance than my liberty. Herod!

BURKE   [*getting angry*]   Keep quiet!

ROBERT   Nero!

BURKE   [*bellowing*]   Shut up!

ROBERT   Shut up yourself! Machiavelli!

BURKE   [*inarticulate with rage*]   I'll—I'll—

ROBERT   Bismarck! Napoleon! Henry the Eighth! Ivan the Terrible! Northcliffe! Rockefeller!

BURKE   [*capitulating*]   Well, well, all right. Go on and say what you have to say and when you've finished give me a chance.

ROBERT   I have nothing to say. But I insist upon my right to freedom of speech.

Although the specific terms of liberalism have changed somewhat, the playlet remains amusing and still holds the boards. In the past five years, it has been produced five times in the United States and once abroad.

Two other pleasant and still-produced one-acts belong to this period. *The Passing of Chow-Chow* is a charming absurdity about a young married couple and their quarrel over the wife's dog. Perhaps the best way to suggest the flavor of the little piece and to recommend it for production is to quote a typical passage.

RUSSELL   And your husband has been ill-treating this— er—animal?

MRS. STANDISH   Yes, he disliked her, from the moment I bought her. He said she reminded him of an overgrown caterpillar. He says the most wicked things sometimes. And poor little Chow-Chow just begs to be loved. She's an orphan, you know. When she was ten days old, her mother was killed by an ambulance, and the week after that her father was vivisected. And once she got into the kitchen and almost lost one of her paws in the meat-chopper. As it was, her little foot was badly bruised.

RUSSELL   I suppose you acquainted your husband with these unfortunate incidents in the life of the animal in question?

MRS. STANDISH   Oh, yes, I told him about it, almost every day. But it only made him hate poor Chow-Chow more. Every time he'd pass an ambulance on the street, he'd take off his hat and bow. And he said it was just his luck that Chow-Chow's mother wasn't killed eleven days sooner. And then, when Chow-Chow injured her paw, he wrote a poem, dedicated to the meat-chopper; and now he's taken the meat-chopper out of the kitchen, and put it on a cushion in his studio, tied with blue ribbon. And he closes the windows carefully every night, because, he says, he doesn't want the meat-chopper to catch cold.

The other one-act, A *Diadem of Snow*, is more important in its theme, and has a Shavian bite to its dialogue. It shows Czar Nicholas II living with his wife and son in Siberia after the Revolution of 1918. The Czar spends his time reading Tolstoy and glorying in a life of labor. When an envoy from the Kaiser offers to put him back on the throne, he refuses because he finds being a worker more healthy, valuable, and satisfying than being Czar. The play was written shortly after the revolution, but before the execution of the Romanovs, and I am not certain how the audience's knowledge of the execution would affect the play. If one can consider the play merely for itself, its wit has lost little of its edge.

Although Rice's one-acts are amusing and successful, he has written few short plays. His reason is that,

the exigencies of the one-act play tend to throw the emphasis upon form rather than upon substance. Technical skill counts for more than the poetic gift; and inventive ingenuity is more telling than the free flowering of inspiration. What is likely to result is a *tour de force:* a pretty mechanical contrivance which, however much it may excite our admiration, is scarcely calculated to induce that emotional catharsis which is presumably the chief function (or, let us say, effect) of art at its best.[8]

iii

In 1916, Rice attended a convention of the National Child Labor Committee in Asheville, North Carolina. On his journey he visited some cotton mills where he was shocked to see "pale, emaciated children of ten and twelve at work in the lint-laden air of the ill-lighted spinning rooms." The result of this experience was *The House in Blind Alley*—a combination of propaganda against child labor and an alternately charming and chilling Mother Goose pantomime. Various producers professed to admire the play, but no one thought enough of its commercial value to stage it. The excuse of Belasco, described by Rice as "that old fraud," was that the use of child actors would violate the child labor laws.

It is a pity that Rice never returned to this vein, for the play is a greater achievement than *On Trial* and the other commercial plays of his apprenticeship. For pure theatricality, I would rank it with *The Adding Machine* and *The Subway* as the best of Rice's early work.

Structurally, the play resembles *On Trial*, with an outer framework and an inner story. We first see John First and his mother and his son Jack. To their home comes John's brother Jules, who wants John to invest in some coal mine stock, although the company employs children. After Jules leaves, a little girl, Ella, is discovered on the back porch. She is the child of a working man and very poor. After she is put to bed, John has a dream which takes up most of the play. In his dream, his son is Jack the Giant Killer, and he and his brother are giants who enslave the children from *Mother Goose's Nursery Rhymes*, make them work in sweatshop conditions, and feed them finally into a large and terrible machine which converts them into loaves of bread. The grandmother appears as Mother Goose and gives Jack her gander and other magic gifts to combat the giants. Nevertheless, Jack is captured, and in a grim final scene the children are fed into the machine, and even Jack and Cinderella die. John then awakens and resolves to put an end to the "giant."

I have not in this summary done justice to the charm, the grimness, or the content of the story. Technically, however, the play is one of the most stage-straining that Rice ever wrote. The curtain which opens the first act prologue represents the cover of a volume of *Mother Goose*. On it is a life-size Mother Goose astride a large gander, and from the book emerge children portraying various Mother Goose characters. The first scene of the act shows us that this book was resting against John's chair, so we then understand why a giant newspaper during the prologue was dropped from above and why a giant hand closed the prologue by reaching down to pick the book up.

Among the play's other appealing theatrical elements are the gander and the young hero fighting giants who are, incidentally, described as "48 feet high and proportionally broad and terrible." Perhaps the finale is a bit fierce by our overly protective modern standards of children's literature, but my own experience is that children are tough creatures who admire Long John Silver more than Little Lord Fauntleroy. The specific theme of child labor is fortunately dated, but in a broader sense the theme will still work, for Jack's duel with the giant is shown to us in terms of the disguise and eventual discovery of hypocrisy. In some form, hypocrisy is perennially with us. Aside from its theme, the story itself has considerable appeal just as a story, and whoever has the honor to resurrect this excellent play and stage it will provide a lively and colorful show.

iv

Between the production of *On Trial* in 1914 and his next significant production, that of *The Adding Machine* in 1923, Rice wrote two kinds of plays: potboilers and what he called "experiments in form, adventures in realism, developments of social and ethical themes." In addition to *The Iron Cross* and *The House in Blind Alley*, he wrote a play, neither published nor produced, called

The Kingdom of Heaven. This he described as "a parable of modern industrial life which closely followed the narrative of the New Testament." In his autobiography, he also describes three unnamed plays.

> I turned back to technical experimentation, developing a formula that was far more intricate than that of *On Trial:* each act of the play set in a different location— several rooms in the same house, for example—and synchronous with the others. The interweaving of incident and the gradual clearing up of the seemingly inexplicable had the fascination of a chess problem. I wrote no fewer than three plays employing this device; wasted effort, for none of them ever aroused the slightest interest. Yet perhaps not altogether wasted, for failure can be instructive. In later years I was able to make more successful experiments. I have never lost my interest in technical innovation, partly to counteract the constricting effect that Ibsen has had upon the drama, partly because I enjoy setting myself puzzles.[9]

Among his potboiling activities was a stint in Hollywood which he said "almost destroyed my capacity for thinking and writing at all." Between 1917 and 1923, he had three potboilers produced in New York. These were *For the Defense* in 1919, *Wake Up, Jonathan* in 1921, and *It Is the Law* in 1922. He described the first and last of these as:

> mystery melodramas, potboilers written in my youth. . . .
> *It is the Law* was a dramatization of an unpublished novel by Hayden Talbot, a newspaperman. *For the Defense* was rewritten and mangled by its star, Richard Bennett. These two plays had moderately good runs in New York, and were made into movies. The only interesting thing about *For the Defense* is that during its run, Bennett cautiously tried out *Beyond the Horizon* at special matinees: O'Neill's first Broadway production.[10]

Wake Up, Jonathan, which was not totally a potboiler, was written with Hatcher Hughes during the days of Rice's involvement with the Morningside Players. Archie Binns' book, *Mrs. Fiske and the American Theatre,* incorrectly suggests that the first draft was written by Hughes and accepted for production by Mrs. Fiske, and only then did Rice come to the script as a kind of play doctor. The correct account is to be found in *Minority Report*. The play was based upon an idea of Hughes, but the script was written by both. They intended the play as a vehicle for David Warfield and offered it to Belasco who ultimately decided against it. During Rice's exile in Hollywood, Hughes placed it with Harrison Grey Fiske as a vehicle for his wife. Hughes consulted with Rice about the revision but did the actual rewriting himself.

The published version is in a prologue and three acts, and the prologue is Hughes' work. Binns remarks that the play, which was called *The Homecoming* in its earlier version, had had a prologue showing a cave woman "hesitating between a down-to-earth cave man and a poet." Apparently this Hughes-Rice prologue contained in embryo the plot of the play itself. The published prologue, which was played by Mrs. Fiske, is set just a few minutes before the opening of Act I and shows one of the main characters returning home.

The story tells how a business tycoon returns home to the family he had left years before, and how he tries to win back their affection. At first, the wife and children reject him in favor of another early beau of their mother, a poet, who has also just returned from his wanderings. The plot centers around the mother's choice, and somewhat surprisingly she chooses the husband, but not before he has had his pretensions punctured and decides that he must change many of his values.

The plot is well managed, but stagey-clever rather than real. The play is about real enough issues, but the characters are drawn in such archly theatrical strokes that they would appear grotesque today. The husband, Jonathan, is a bald stereotype of the capitalist, and this broad character drawing gives the play a ruinous aura of theatricality. Nevertheless, because of Mrs. Fiske's popularity, the play had a mildly successful run. Of it, Rice remarked, "Except for keeping my name alive in the theatre, it gave me little satisfaction." There would be little point in reviving this relic today.

v

From his apprentice years on Broadway and in Hollywood, Rice learned that commercial success depends as much upon luck as upon craftsmanship. Rice's first potboiler was the artistic and commercial success of the 1914–15 season, but he was also during this time writing a succession of theatrical experiments whose production would have notably hastened the birth of the modern American drama. None of these experiments reached the commercial stage, and for nine years Rice only reached the New York stage in either amateur productions or in trivial potboilers. This must have been a depressing experience that confirmed in him the belief that the commercial theatre was a timid, intellectually impoverished endeavor.

The Adding Machine, first produced by the Theatre Guild in March, 1923, is probably Rice's most performed and best known play, but its first production received a mixed press. Even the favorable notices were unenthusiastic, and Ludwig Lewisohn was almost alone in claiming that play and production were a major achievement in American theatre. Looking back on this production forty years later, Rice remarked, "I had no reason to be dissatisfied. A first-rate production, substantial recognition, a nine-week run: it was all more than could have been reasonably expected. Today it would be impossible to find a Broadway producer for the play—the cost of presentation alone would be a deterrent."[1] One consoling fact about the career of *The Adding Machine* is that a half-hearted commercial reception did not kill the play. "There is hardly a community or university theatre in the English-speaking world," remarked Rice, "that has not produced it at one time or another. . . . Whatever the reasons, the play's survival has been a bright spot in a career that has not been without defeats and frustrations."[2] The play's survival is also encouraging proof that the amateur theatre can function, if it will, as a court of appeal from Broadway.

In *Minority Report,* Rice surmises that the play's continued popularity derives from the spread of automation and its own stylized technique which would be intriguing in our predominantly realistic theatre. Perhaps another reason is that it manages to be stylized without puzzling or alienating its audience. Its cast is relatively small, and, even though the original production had complicated sets, the staging need not be elaborate. Perhaps still another reason is that Rice's indictment in this play is as much psychological as social, and is therefore less tied to a particular social problem, political issue, or period of modern history.

A main reason, certainly, for the play's continued popularity is that it is comic, and its indictment of Zero is presented partly through the indirection of irony and satire. An intellectual distance is maintained between the audience and Zero. Without totally identifying ourselves with him, we see portions of ourselves in him. We indict the Zero mentality and presumably by some mental osmosis become less like Zero. This method, at least, is the classic explanation of comedy, and this discussion will stress a point that has been insufficiently made about the play: in form, content, intention, and effect, it is a satiric comedy, and its hero a comic character.

Zero's worthlessness is indicated in many ways—by his speech and actions, by overt statement of the other characters, and by the entire plot. Perhaps at first he does not seem totally worthless, despite his name, for an audience would have some sympathy for a man harnessed to a woman like Mrs. Zero. Some of this sympathy may remain even when Zero kills his boss, for we should feel for a man rebelling against the blind impersonality of a system. Having established this much identification with Zero, Rice then lashes into his character in the trial scene and the Elysian Fields scene. Zero's zestful savagery in the first and his inability to accept human fulfillment in the second both strikingly clinch Rice's point of Zero's basic worthlessness. The play is, despite its amusing satire, a grim and black comedy dissecting the soul of machine-conditioned man and finding nothing there. The Adding Machine has reduced modern man to a Zero, and the final remark of the play—"Hell, I'll tell the world this is a lousy job!"—is a bitterly apt fillip to end on.

Despite the starkness of the indictment, it is much to the credit of the play that it has been appreciated. It is easy for a comic writer taking a sardonic and nihilistic view to drive his audience away. To a considerable extent, Shakespeare drove his audience away in *Timon of Athens* and Molière did in *The Misanthrope*. If one can retain such a view and one's audience, one has accomplished something indeed. The viewpoint in such plays bursts the boundaries of comedy into fierce indignation, and this Swiftean attitude wars with the traditional manner, the control, of comedy itself.

The play is saved by its technical dexterity. Its devices allow for surprise and pleasure that make its ferocity palatable. One device, the monologue, is especially instructive for modern dramatists. In Scenes One and Four, Rice has written two of the longest and best monologues of the modern drama. Realism has nearly driven the monologue and the soliloquy from the boards, yet some dramatic devices we scrap to our detriment. In unrealistic plays, the soliloquy furthered the plot, probed the mind, and allowed an exhibition of the art of acting. In most modern realistic plays, there is a crying need for what the soliloquy used to do. Most modern plays which attempt the soliloquy do it awkwardly or apologetically, as in the "Attention must be paid" speech of *Death of a Salesman*. Shaw's remark that plays should exhibit the art of acting is a half-truth worth remembering, but with the monosyllables of the modern drama the range of acting is restricted. The soliloquy, in the hands of a good actor, can intensify the emotional effect of a play immensely, and those few modern dramatists who have not avoided the extended speech will surely be among those most remembered.

The two long speeches of *The Adding Machine* are of high theatrical excellence. Here is a short typical excerpt from the first, by Mrs. Zero.

. . . But it's my own fault, I guess. I was a fool for marryin' you. If I'd 'a' had any sense, I'd 'a' known what you were from the start. I wish I had it to do over again, I hope to tell you. You was goin' to do wonders, you was! You wasn't goin' to be a bookkeeper long—oh, no, not you. Wait till you got started—you was goin' to show 'em. There wasn't no job in the store that was too big for you. Well, I've been waitin'—waitin' for you to get started— see? It's been a good long wait too. Twenty-five years! An' I ain't seen nothin' happen. Twenty-five years in the same job. Twenty-five years tomorrow! You're proud of it, ain't you? Twenty-five years in the same job an' never missed a day! That's somethin' to be proud of, ain't it? Sittin' for twenty-five years on the same chair, addin' up figures.

This monologue works upon the page, but it demands speech, for much of its effect depends upon the beautiful variations of exasperation that an actress gives to the constant repetition of a single idea. It must be a repetition stressing that each rephrasal is to her not a rephrasal but almost a new discovery of bitterness. On the page, the speech evokes a mild amusement, but on the stage it would evoke rueful laughter. It is a speech that pulses with the dull, accumulated exasperation that one may hear in suburbia today. It jolts an audience with a gasp of recognition, for it contains that pervasive, impotent, and inarticulate rage against life that rises from our culture. Many expressionistic plays hit the audience immediately with strangeness and unreality; Rice's play catches its audience immediately with what Edmund Wilson called the shock of recognition. After this initial delight, the author may perform almost what technical hijinks he will, for he has captured his audience.

The second long speech is Zero's explanation to the jury in Scene Four. Here Rice cannot depend upon mere recognition, for the situation is not typical. Yet this speech works even better than Mrs. Zero's.

Sure I killed him. I ain't sayin' I didn't, am I? Sure I killed him. Them lawyers! They give me a good stiff pain, that's what they give me. Half the time I don't know what the hell they're talkin' about. Objection sustained. Objection overruled. What's the big idea anyhow? You ain't heard me do any objectin', have you? Sure not! What's the idea of objectin'? You got a right to know. What I say is, if one bird kills another bird, why you got a right to call him for it. That's what I say. I know all about that. I been on the jury too. Them lawyers! Don't let 'em fill you full of bunk. All that bull about it bein' red ink on the bill file. Red ink nothin'! It was blood, see? I want you to get that right. I killed him, see? Right through the heart with the bill file, see? I want you to get that right—all of you. One, two, three, four, five, six, seven, eight, nine, ten, eleven, twelve. Twelve of you. Six and six. That makes twelve. I figgered it up often enough. Six and six makes twelve. And five is seventeen. And eight is twenty-five. And three is twenty-eight. Eight and carry two. Aw, cut it out! Them damn figgers! I can't forget 'em. Twenty-five years, see. Eight hours a day, exceptin' Sundays. And July and August half-day Saturday. One week's vacation with pay. And another week without pay if you want it. Who the hell wants it? Layin' around the house listenin' to the wife tellin' you where you get off. Nix! An' legal holidays. I nearly forget them. New Year's, Washington's Birthday, Decoration Day, Fourth o' July, Labor Day, Election Day, Thanksgivin', Christmas. Good Friday if you want it. An' if you're a Jew, Young Kipper an' the other one—I forget what they call it. The dirty sheenies—always gettin' two to the other bird's one.

Rice has the same problem here that O'Neill often faced, but could not always solve—the problem of conveying the feelings of a person who is barely articulate. O'Neill, like Rice, used colloquial speech, but with a great deal more slang. Indeed, in some plays, even in the superb *The Iceman Cometh*, slang becomes the chief part of the characters' vocabulary. Since much of O'Neill's slang has become dated, there seems a quaint awkwardness about much of his dialogue.

There are but two slang expressions in Zero's speech, "bunk" and "bull," and this is scarcely a large enough proportion to give the speech its main flavor. Rice suggests Zero's character by using fragments and by eliding some of the words. Also, as Rice chooses Zero's vocabulary from the simple stockpile of basic words, the speech seems less a relic of former times than does much of O'Neill's dialogue.

Rice also uses the principle of association; one word or thought sets Zero off in certain channelled tangents, and he must by an effort bring himself back to his subject. Usually, a reference to a number sets Zero off on a conditioned-response tabulation of meaningless digits. And, as the subject is Zero's own life or death, Rice makes his point neatly about Zero's zombie-like intelligence.

Seldom in the speech does Rice allow the audience to feel pity. The remark about Jews alienates sympathy, and later Zero gets sidetracked into discussing a lynching. "Boy, I'd of liked to been there, with a gat in each hand, pumpin' him full of lead." (This insight into mass man was thirty years later to sell millions of books for Mickey Spillane.) What Rice wants in this play is not easy compassion for an individual, but horror at a system which creates Zeros.

Another effective device in the play is the aside. We see it in Scene Two when Zero and Daisy are working together. Sometimes they speak directly to each other, but more often they give their thoughts aloud as asides. "During the asides," Rice remarked to me, "the other character kept intoning numbers, *sotto voce*. Very effective! But impossible to convey, of course, on the printed page." In this dialogue we get such effectively ironic counterpoint as:

ZERO   Was the last you said eighty-seven dollars?
DAISY   [*consulting the slip*]   Forty-two fifty.
ZERO   Well, I made a mistake. Wait a minute. [*He busies himself with an eraser.*] All right. Shoot.
DAISY   Six dollars. Three fifteen. Two twenty-five. Sixty-five cents. A dollar twenty. You talk to me as if I was dirt.
ZERO   I wonder if I could kill the wife without anybody findin' out. In bed some night. With a pillow.
DAISY   I used to think you was stuck on me.
ZERO   I'd get found out though. They always have ways.
DAISY   We used to be so nice and friendly together when I first came here. You used to talk to me then.
ZERO   Maybe she'll die soon. I noticed she was coughin' this mornin'.

In Scene Three Rice has written a brilliant modern adaptation of the chorus. After an apt collection of clichés spouted out in chorus by Messrs. One, Two, Three, Four, Five, Six, and their wives, there comes this fierce outburst, with all shouting in unison:

> That's it! Damn foreigners! Damn dagoes! Damn Catholics! Damn sheenies! Damn niggers! Jail 'em! Shoot 'em! Hang 'em all! Lynch 'em! Burn 'em! [*They all rise . . . sing in unison:*]
> "*My country 'tis of thee,*
> *Sweet land of liberty!*"

The growing rhythmic intensity culminates in the theatrical jolt of the song and gives to this mordant scene a climax of great impact.

Besides his adaptation of the traditional devices of soliloquy, aside, and chorus, Rice surprises his audience with the effective fantasy of the graveyard and Elysian Fields scenes, before ending with the supreme example of Zero's unimportance—the example of how his soul is used and re-used as a kind of spiritual carbon paper. The celestial adding machine of the last scene, with its billowing strip of paper, is reminiscent of the stage-filling machine in *The House in Blind Alley*, and shows that Zero has a really cosmic unimportance. The last scene tops what Rice had said before; it makes his theme starker and blacker.

The Adding Machine deserves the appreciation it has received. The combination of traditional devices and modern expressionism remains still fresh and theatrical. The satire has lost none of its edge. If the theme is as black as Gulliver's final view of the Yahoos, the whole play is yet well enough wrought to triumph over its theme. The only play that Rice wrote better in this vein was the equally deft but more affirmitive satire, *The Subway*.

ii

The Subway was written shortly after *The Adding Machine*, in 1923. Like the earlier satire, it did not intrigue commercial managements. It was accepted for production by several groups, but each finally dropped it, and it had to wait until 1929 for an amateur production in Greenwich Village. Rice thought, "The production, though far below the best professional standards, was creditable enough." The *New York Times* thought the production "uncertain," but the reviews were sufficiently encouraging for William A. Brady, whose production of *Street Scene* had recently opened, to move *The Subway* to Broadway, where it soon closed.

The Subway is in the same manner as *The Adding Machine* and has a similar theme. In *The Adding Machine*, Rice took a mechanized device as his central symbol, and showed how the mechanized world had produced a Zero mentality; in *The Subway*, he again uses a mechanical contraption for his central symbol to show how human life and aspiration are minimized. Again, the human is slave to the machine, and this metallic impersonality of the modern world is well caught in the steel and concrete of the play's first scene in the subway office. The second and final scenes use the subway in more meaningfully dramatic terms than the adding machine had been used. These scenes require an excellent staging for their full theatrical effect, but with such a staging their adroit blending of sound, movement, and color should easily equal anything in the earlier play. The second scene shows the platform of a moving subway train, on which the heroine is standing.

> The train is moving. One hears the rush and rumble of it, the rattling of the chains that link the cars, the grinding of a flat wheel, the occasional tooting of a whistle. There is a rapid, regular alternation of lights, as the train sweeps by the lamps affixed to the walls of the tunnel.

The platform is crowded with frightening-looking people.

> A thin man, with sharp nose and chin, beady eyes and a straggly moustache. A man with flaring nostrils and fangs and cruel eyes. A man with a grinning, hairy face. . . . One or two shout inarticulately above the din. But for the

most part, they stand silent, immobile, staring vacuously, imbecilely.

When the train stops, there is a savage rush for the doors. Police fiercely tear some of them away, and as the train moves off again with a deafening roar the heroine is crushed tight among the people on the platform.

> But they all wear masks now; hideous, grotesque, animal masks: a dog, a pig, a monkey, a wolf, a rat.
> [*She turns her head, sees them, sees the animal faces. A shriek.*] BLACKNESS.

This strong theatrical scene makes quite unnecessary any overt statement of the theme of the play, that the symbolic subway drains the humanity from people and reduces them to beasts.

Rice's attitude toward his theme is different, however, from what it was in *The Adding Machine*. The earlier play was a dark, caustic comedy with no compassion for the Zeros of the world. In this play, the heroine is a young girl, Sophie Smith, who works in the filing office of the subway company, and Rice has much compassion for her. Her destruction by the subway in the last scene is presented as a waste, a pathetic loss, almost a tragedy. Rice's view of the modern world is still scathingly critical, but his new play is much more than a satire.

The character and the story of Sophie Smith seem to refute that view, propagated by Joseph Wood Krutch, that tragedy is impossible in our time. According to Krutch's view, modern man has been too minimized by his world to be important enough for tragedy. Sophie is admittedly a little person. She has no great abilities, and she is not especially intelligent. Still, her loss is moving and important, for she has the important human desires for love and affection. These desires give her an importance and a stature. Her humanity—her ability to feel love and anguish—makes her important.

Actually, there is a similarity between her story and the pattern of classical tragedy. Sophie has no chance of success; her struggle is foredoomed because what she is fighting is too big, too implacable, too inexorable. Her antagonist is the industrial society of the present, but Rice gives that society some of the qualities which were in classical tragedies given to the gods or to fate. We find the same kind of opposition in Aeschylus' *Prometheus Bound*; just as Prometheus dared to struggle, though conscious of ultimate failure and punishment, so does Sophie struggle in her attempt to attain love and happiness. "I didn't do anything I didn't want to do," she says.

She is as much a victim as is Willy Loman or Studs Lonigan, but she is not nearly so blind and yielding. The Lomans and Lonigans of modern literature are trapped and impotent and baffled, totally formed by society and only dimly aware of their plight, characters ultimately too feeble to pit their wills against their environment. Rice's Sophie is not such a character; she has a will. Rice has said that the central theme of all his serious plays is freedom, and Milton, an author whom Rice knows well, has remarked that freedom is but choosing. In other words, the value of literature in any age is finally posited upon the value of man's free will. In *The Subway* and in Rice's other serious plays that value is dramatized and affirmed, and that fact gives to his plays a dignity and an importance.

Technically, *The Subway* is most interesting. Scene 3, for instance, uses a quite effective device. In this scene, Sophie brings home Eugene, the young artist who is interested in her. Her mother is ironing, and her father and brother are reading the newspaper. As Sophie and Eugene chat, the mother continues to iron, and the father and brother mechanically read out items from the paper: "Steel Trust Cuts Twenty-Seven—Million—Dollar Melon"; "Giants May Clinch Flag Tomorrow"; "Eli's Gridiron Outlook Bright, Says Dooley." And interspersed also is the sound of the derisive cuckoo-clock, the traditional sound of mockery. The apathy of the mother, father, and brother is neatly caught in this short, stylized scene.

Especially effective also should be the fifth scene in the balcony of a motion picture theatre. As Sophie and

Eugene sit watching the film, they occasionally talk to each other, but more often they speak out loud to themselves. Eugene is amused and impressed by her naïveté, and she is alternately entranced by what is happening on the screen and conscious of him touching her. Throughout, there is an ironic counterpointing of the spuriously sentimental sentiments in the film's story of seduction and the actual beginning of Sophie's seduction:

SOPHIE "Meanwhile Masters despairingly prepared to return to London."
EUGENE No! I won't! [*He takes his hand away again.*]
SOPHIE "Shure and it's sorry we'll be to see you go, sir." . . . Oh, God, why don't you let me die?
EUGENE No!
[*With mechanical deliberation, he takes her hand in his. She submits passively, without any attempt at resistance.*]
SOPHIE I oughtn't to let him.
EUGENE What's happening to me? It's incredible. . . . A little shop-girl.
SOPHIE "Suspecting nothing, Kathleen walks into the trap set for her by Lord Orville.". . . His knee . . . I oughtn't to let him.

The diction of the play is simple, but its use of the trite phrase and of short terse sentences is appropriate as literature and effective as theatre. This diction works well, as it did in *The Adding Machine*, in a soliloquy. There is a fine, pathetic soliloquy in the fourth scene, in which Sophie in her bedroom begs God for warmth and love. This scene should be impressive in the hands of a capable actress.

Sophie's reaching out for love is continually blocked by her world, and reaches its culmination in the final scene, in which she leaps off the subway platform to embrace the onrushing train. Her speech describes the train in the same tone that her earlier speeches had described her lover.

It's rushing along, now. Look at it rushing, rushing along. Oh, it's so beautiful. It's so beautiful. I never knew it was so beautiful. Oh Eugene, Eugene! Listen to it! Look at the lights. Red like blood. I'm shaking, Eugene. Like when you kiss me—like when you take me in your arms. I'm so happy—I'm so happy. I want to die. Kiss me, Eugene, kiss me until I die.

Using the light and sound of the approaching train, the scene builds to a harrowing crescendo, and superbly makes Rice's point about the ultimate rape of humanity and the mechanization of human feeling in the modern world. Sophie, like Willy Loman, is killed by the machine, but Miller merely relates an offstage death, while Rice builds his play to it. For plot construction, for immediacy of impact, as well as for the implications loved by symbol hunters, *The Subway* is a theatrical, a masterly, a daring play. Its ending is fiercer and blacker than the ending of *The Adding Machine*, but Rice has added to it the extra dimension of compassion. He has given to *The Subway* the pattern of tragedy.

iii

Rice wrote in this period no more significant work that reached the stage. He did take an extended trip to Europe, he suffered a serious illness, and he worked on four unimportant plays which were staged. Two of these plays were adaptations and two were collaborations.

One of these plays, *The Mongrel*, Rice describes as not even an adaptation, but "a routine job" of play-doctoring. The original translation was made by another person from a German play of Herman Bahr, and Rice merely smoothed out the dialogue. The play appeared in New York in late 1924 as a vehicle for Rudolph Schildkraut and lasted for only thirty-two performances. *The Blue Hawaii* was an adaptation of a German play by Rudolf Lothar, which Rice undertook for Sam Harris. Of it, Rice remarked, "The play dealt with the mysterious disappearance of a rare postage stamp, to which the title referred. I think there was a murder in it, too. It was another of those exercises in dramatic technique that I seem unable to resist." [3] The play opened and closed in Boston. Neither adaptation has been published.

The collaborations are more interesting, and both have been published. The first was written with Dorothy Parker. According to *Minority Report,* she had written a first act which "was as long as an entire play, and completely formless." Rice concentrated on shaping the play and developing the plot. After he and Miss Parker had minutely discussed the action of a scene, she wrote most of the dialogue. The play was called *Close Harmony* and was produced in New York by Philip Goodman and Arthur Hopkins on December 1, 1924. It received mildly favorable notices, but lasted only thirty-two performances. It was more successful on the road where, with the title of *The Lady Next Door,* it ran for twenty-five weeks.

The play is a mild satire on suburban dullness. The hero is an uninteresting, inoffensive man plagued by an intolerable wife, a harridan of a sister-in-law, and a viper of a young daughter. Next door lives an attractive young wife, an ex-chorus girl whose husband has grown tired of her. The hero and the lady next door are drawn together by mutual loneliness and probably because they are the only moderately decent people around. They decide to run away together, but at the last moment a minor accident to the hero's daughter makes him decide that he cannot desert his family no matter how awful they are. However, his experience with the lady next door has emboldened him to assert himself as the man of the house.

The plot is simple, and the characterizations are flat. The three female relatives are adequately differentiated stage types, the older women being nagging harpies and the child a spoiled brat. Although effective enough as humors, they are so broadly drawn that their satiric point is dulled. *Close Harmony* is really a dull play about dull people. Such a theme and such characters require either more sympathy or more satire. There is some sympathy for the husband, but he is not made as important as Sophie Smith or as interesting as Zero. There is no sympathy for Suburbia, which is painted as dull, narrow, and pedestrian. The view is valid enough, but the treatment should not partake of the theme's dullness. A Sinclair Lewis was really needed to do the theme justice. Miss Parker is, of course, well known for her acid pen, and Rice proved in *The Adding Machine* and in *A Voyage to Purilia*, his satiric novel about the movies, that he too could write with wit and bite. Little of the authors' satiric ability is apparent in the script, and for this reason the play received pretty much the success it deserved.

Rice's second collaboration was a comic mystery play *Cock Robin*, which he wrote with another wit of the period, Philip Barry. The plot is rather ingenious, but the characters are unmemorable. What is most interesting is the novelty of the setting. The play occurs on the stage of a little theatre during a rehearsal and a performance of a costume play. The first act shows how the various characters dislike one of the actors, Hancock Robinson. The second act occurs during the performance and opens with a fine business report about the theatre's activities and finances. During this act, Robinson is killed onstage, and the third act runs through the play a third time, in order to reconstruct the crime. The play within a play device remains perennially fresh, and the authors make the same scene interesting, even though we see it played three different times. The setting is also freshly handled. In Act I, the stage is seen from the front of the theatre, but in Acts II and III we see it from behind—the same device that e. e. cummings used in *Him*.

During rehearsals, Barry's attention was primarily engaged by Arthur Hopkins' imminent production of his *Paris Bound*, and Rice had difficulty in securing permission to make necessary revisions of *Cock Robin*. In *Minority Report*, Rice remarked about the production:

> *Cock Robin* managed to survive in New York for a hundred performances; but that was far short of everybody's expectations. We had all been sure that there would be spirited bidding for the motion picture rights, yet not a single offer was ever made. For Barry, with his glittering success, the indifferent showing of *Cock Robin* meant little. As I remember it, he did not even stay for the New York opening. For me it was another setback. I had no

great pride of authorship, but I had believed that the play would ease my economic pressures.

iv

In 1925, Rice wrote an interesting experiment which remained unproduced and only published in part. Called *The Sidewalks of New York*, it seems an appropriate conclusion to this chapter, for in several ways it was the forerunner of his next play, the Pulitzer Prize winning *Street Scene*. In *Minority Report*, Rice described *The Sidewalks of New York* as:

> another technical experiment: a play without words; not a pantomime, in which speech is indicated by gesture, but a series of situations in which there was no need for speech. It dealt with the struggles of a boy and a girl who come separately to New York to make their own way. . . . It contained a series of episodes illustrative of various phases of New York life, linked only by the passage of the same set of characters through them. Some of the scenes were realistic, some symbolic, some expressionistic. The intended total effect was a panoramic impression of New York.

When the play was rejected by the Theatre Guild, Rice made little further attempt to market it. However, some of its scenes found their way into print, and it is possible to get an idea of what the play was like.

"Exterior," like *Street Scene*, occurs in front of a brownstone apartment house, and shows the house awakening in the morning. This scene, in fact, became the opening of Act II of *Street Scene*. Although its details are well chosen, its lack of a story prevents it from being more than a dramatic exercise. The three other published scenes have stories, and thus more of dramatic interest. Each little story ends on a peak of emotion—the wryly rueful, the romantically expectant, or the poignantly disappointing. On paper, the stories seem little more than O'Henry-ish vignettes, but I believe that on a stage they would work. There has been little use of mime in the modern drama, and it is a pity that Rice's experiment remained unproduced. Offhand, I can think of only one other modern dramatist who has made such an attempt, but not even Samuel Beckett has tried a full length play. Indeed, Beckett's little plays without words are all in one manner, but, according to a letter from Rice, at least half of the scenes of *The Sidewalks of New York* "are, in whole or in part, fantasy or expressionistic." [4] Three of the published scenes are provocative exercises in the art of acting, and suggest that one more fascinating play has been lost for the modern repertoire by the timidity of commercial managements.

Street Scene was produced in 1929, ran for 602 per-formances, won the Pulitzer Prize, and is one of the great plays of the American theatre. It had the longest Broadway run of any of Rice's plays, and, with the exception of the London production of *Judgment Day*, it gave him prob-ably the greatest satisfaction. The tragicomic history of the play is fascinatingly told in Chapter XIX of *The Living Theatre* and Chapter XIII of *Minority Report*. Of special interest is the difficulty that Rice had in marketing the script.

> The responses of the producers were emphatically and unanimously negative. I remember some of them. The Theatre Guild, which had produced my play *The Adding Machine*, said that *Street Scene* had "no content." Win-throp Ames, a man for whose judgment I had great re-spect, said that it was not a play. Arthur Hopkins, who had scored a great success with my first play, *On Trial*, told me that he found *Street Scene* unreadable. Others found it dull, depressing, sordid, confusing, undramatic. One pro-ducer opened the script, looked at the list of characters and read no further.[1]

It seems astonishing that so many astute authorities could have been so wrong; still, a book could be filled with similar cases. If any generalization is to be drawn from such facts, it might be that the commercial theatre imposes its own standards upon those who work in it. When money is the first consideration, safety is the second and quality is the last. Of the play itself, Rice once wrote:

> The background and subject matter had been in my mind for many years: a multiple dwelling, housing numerous families of varying origins; and a melodramatic story arising partly from the interrelationships of the characters and partly from their environmental conditioning. The setting was the façade of a "brownstone front"—a type of dwelling of which there are still thousands of examples in New York—and the sidewalk before it. . . . The house was conceived as the central fact of the play: a dominant structural element that unified the sprawling and diversified lives of the inhabitants. This concept was derived partly from the Greek drama, which is almost always set against the face of a palace or a temple. But mainly I was influenced, I think, by the paintings of Claude Lorrain, a French artist of the seventeenth century. In his landscapes, which I had gazed at admiringly in the Louvre and other galleries, there is nearly always a group of figures in the foreground, which is composed and made significant by an impressive architectural pile of some sort in the background. In fact, the original title of my play was *Landscape with Figures*; but I felt that this was a little too special, so I borrowed again from the terminology of painting and called the play *Street Scene*. . . .
>
> There is a central love story: a sort of Romeo and Juliet romance between the stagehand's daughter and the radical's son; and a main dramatic thread of murder, committed by the girl's father when he comes home unexpectedly and finds his wife with her lover. But there are numerous subplots and an intricate pattern of crisscrossing and interweaving relationships. The house is ever present and ever dominant, and the entire action of the play takes place on the sidewalk, on the stoop or in the windows. I give these details in order to make it clear that, whatever the play's merits or defects, it is an unconventional drama, in setting, in technique and in size of cast.[2]

The problem of discussing this large and unconventional play is that, in one sense, it is too large to discuss. So much happens and there are so many characters, that one scarcely knows where or how to begin. On the other hand, if one stands further back for a broader view, there seems curiously little to discuss. From the welter of incidents, ultimately emerges one simple story, and the rest is scene painting. So viewed, the whole conception seems simplicity itself.

Although the play is realistic, its realism has seldom been seen on the stage since the days of such sprawling Elizabethan plays as *Bartholomew Fair*. It is a realism that suddenly makes one understand with a sort of shock that experiments in realism are still possible. The realism bequeathed by Ibsen was the portrayal of a middle-class drawing room, a front parlor inhabited by half a dozen people. A play like Rice's takes the theatre out of that parlor and sets it down in the middle of a busy metropolitan street. The effect is as if a slab of reality had been hurled at the audience, as if realism itself were abruptly revitalized and its true possibilities beginning at last to be explored.

Compared with *Street Scene*, the front parlor drama seems unreal, contrived, and artificial. It is as if the front parlor dramatists had been using the delicately honed scalpel of realism to extract the meat from nuts rather than the pith from life. Perhaps it is wrong to forget a lesson from Ibsen's own front parlor drama, *A Doll's House*. At the end of that play, its heroine stormed from the house and into the street. And, indeed, most of Ibsen's later plays —*Rosmersholm, John Gabriel Borkman, The Master Builder, The Lady From the Sea*, and *When We Dead Awaken*—all finally escape from the parlor, into the sea, the mountains, and the air. The man who wrote *Brand* and *Peer Gynt* did not regard realism as a confinement, but as the quickest way to freedom. The free realism of *Street Scene* seems to prove the vitality of that realistic form from which so many lesser playwrights have found "No Exit."

I am not suggesting a return to the mere spectacle for spectacle's sake so dear to the heart of Boucicault, but merely suggesting that the modern stage rarely uses its full resources, and that the large cast and the small spectacle performed by real people may be one realization of the theatre at its most vital. *Street Scene* is as pertinent a reminder as *Endgame* or *The Chairs* of what the theatre can do if it will but extend itself. Really, *Street Scene*, with its cast of eighty, may even beat the movies at their own game of spectacle. The eighty-odd characters of *Street Scene* are there, immediate, palpable, tangible; and the effect of real people over colored shadows (no matter how clearly one can see the cleavages in their Brobdingnagian bosoms) is so much more vivid, that eighty real people may dwarf thousands of celluloid shadows.

In the nineteenth-century theatre, actors were accustomed to play types, character types and national types. In our post-Stanislavskian stress upon individual characterization, we may have forgotten a value of the older practice which was, after all, effective, economical, and based upon legitimate observation. *Street Scene* has many national types in its cast—Jews, Italians, Scandinavians, Irish, and so on, and much of the play's effect comes from the delineation and juxtaposition of these types. The jangling cacophony of their dialects, fusing with the diverse street noises, creates a convincing harmony of reality. Such roles not only provide valuable exercises for actors caught in a morass of subtlety, but also allow individual characters to be built up with an economy of effort. Consider, for instance, the effect that Rice gets from a mere stage movement in this exchange between the extroverted Italian Lippo and his German wife.

MRS. FIORENTINO   Lippo, what do you think? Mr. Buchanan has a little girl.
LIPPO   Ah, dotsa fine! Margherita, why you don' have da baby, ha?
MRS. FIORENTINO   [*abruptly*]   I must go and make the coffee.

With similar economy, Rice builds up the characterizations of his large cast, so that his play requires both considerable excellence from each actor and an ensemble playing difficult to achieve.

One character who benefits greatly from this economy

and rings particularly true is the Irish father, Maurrant. His black savagery is clearly caught by the simple repetitions which Rice allows him.

> Who's been sayin' things to you?
> Shut up your swearin', do you hear?—or I'll give you somethin' to bawl for. What did he say to you, huh? What did he say to you?
> Nobody's askin' you? . . . What did he say? . . . G'wan up to bed now, an' don't let me hear no more out o' you. [*Raising his hand*] G'wan now. Beat it.

The theme is expressed with similar economy in several dialogues between Rose Maurrant and Sam Kaplan, the young Jewish student. It is probably, however, the part of the play that suffers most by blunt and economical statement. Most bluntly, it is stated in this interchange from Act I.

SAM   That's all there is in life—nothing but pain. From before we're born, until we die! Everywhere you look, oppression and cruelty! If it doesn't come from Nature, it comes from humanity—humanity trampling on itself and tearing at its own throat. The whole world is nothing but a blood-stained arena, filled with misery and suffering. It's too high a price to pay for life—life isn't worth it!

ROSE   Oh, I don't know, Sam. I feel blue and discouraged sometimes, too. And I get a sort of feeling of, oh, what's the use. Like last night. I hardly slept all night, on account of the heat and on account of thinking about —well, all sorts of things. And this morning, when I got up, I felt so miserable. Well, all of a sudden, I decided I'd walk to the office. And when I got to the Park, everything looked so green and fresh, that I got a feeling of, well, maybe it's not so bad, after all.

The events of the whole play can be seen in these terms, as examples of unfeeling brutality or of sympathy and compassion. Or, to put it another way, as examples of worthlessness and worth, or even of comedy and tragedy. The inhabitants of the tenement help each other, but they also tear at each other. For example, here are the last two speeches of the play, the first compassionate and the second callous.

MISS CUSHING   The poor little thing!

MRS. JONES   Well, you never can tell with them quiet ones. It wouldn't surprise me a bit if she turned out the same way as her mother. She's got a gentleman friend that I guess ain't hangin' around for nothin'. I seen him, late last night, and this afternoon, when I come home from the police.

This dramatization of compassion and brutality is more effective than the overt statement in the interchange between Sam and Rose. Further, just as Mrs. Jones's speech is much longer than Miss Cushing's, so do the brutal events come to outweigh the compassionate ones. There is more of geniality and humor in the first act than in the second, and the last act is relieved only sporadically from grimness. In this increasing darkness of tone, the play resembles the tragicomedies of Gorky and O'Casey and perhaps of Chekhov.

The compassion in the play establishes the worth and humanity of the characters. The brutality does not erase that worth, but makes the plight of these people even more poignant. Rice is not laying the blame on a narrow social basis. He is not condemning a particular society or a certain system of economics for the lives of his people. One of his characters, Abraham Kaplan, does make such a condemnation, but Rice makes it clear that Kaplan is not his *raisonneur*. Rice is not expounding socialism, but human nature, and his play seems to prove that people inevitably destroy themselves, that they carry in themselves the seeds of their own brutality. Without wishing to, they cannot avoid hurting each other. Even Maurrant, who is driven to kill his wife, cries out in agony that he had not meant to. There is no character, except perhaps one outsider, the social worker, who is basically unsympathetic—not even the bullying Irishman Vincent Jones, not even Rose's boss Harry Easter, who is trying to seduce her. Even the savage Maurrant is a basically sympathetic man driven by his own human nature. He is a mixture of brutality and compassion, and the brutality overwhelms the good. This triumph of brutality over compassion is probably the basic theme of the play—a generalization about the human condition, about the nature of man.

Many critics called the play, or at least the story of Maurrant, a melodrama. In the usual sense of the term, melodrama seems inappropriate. One way in which tragedy is usually distinguished from melodrama is by the thickness of characterization. While Maurrant is not a memorable character, as are Hamlet and Othello, he is certainly more valid than the Scarlet Pimpernel or even Sydney Carton. Further, one may plausibly argue that the thinness of his character is filled out by the other characterizations in the play. None is fully drawn, but none is false, and the group to which Maurrant belongs is memorable in the same way that the hero of a tragedy is memorable. Also, the theme of Maurrant's story is acted out in other forms by most of the other characters. Ultimately we get a group as hero, rather as we do in Hauptmann's *The Weavers* or Toller's *Man and the Masses*. The greatest difference is that Rice's group hero is considerably more individualized than Toller's and even more than Hauptmann's.

The importance of the theme, however, is the strongest reason why one may not dismiss *Street Scene* as melodrama. The essence of melodrama is that the theme be unimportant, or at least stated in such heroic or sentimental or platitudinous terms that we do not have to take it seriously, and may therefore concentrate upon an exciting series of events. The theme of *Street Scene* is emphasized by its plot, and is in itself valid and moving. Really, the theme is the same as that of great tragedy and tragicomedy, and this fact seems established by the extent to which the play deeply moved its audiences.

If this notion is true, then the play is one further refutation of Krutch's theory that tragedy is impossible in the modern world. All that is necessary for tragedy is the affirmation of human value. By the compassion of its statement, *Street Scene* establishes that value. Actually, one might take this argument further without unduly stretching it: if one were to judge the play by the classic values of tragedy, it would stand up well. If we take the story of the Maurrant family to be the main story of the play, then the other characters provide an enormous chorus. If we apply the scale of beauty of language, we could even make a case, although some of the dialogue may at first seem flat and bald. The quotations above from Sam and Rose seem naïve and awkward, if compared to any purple passage from Sophocles or Shakespeare. Rice is admittedly not a poet, but the flatness of the Sam-Rose dialogue arises not so much from a limitation of Rice's talent, as from a limitation of realistic dialogue. Of this fact, he himself is quite conscious, as we shall see in *Not for Children*, where he satirizes the attempt of the realistic writer to rise above flat statement to beauty or poetry.

We must consider also that speech in a play is more than words and their meanings and overtones; it is also the sound of words. One of Shaw's most valid criticisms of the Shakespearean productions of the 1890's was that they extracted the meaning from Shakespeare while butchering the "word music." Even the Sam-Rose dialogue, when spoken with the right tone, expression, and dialects, provides beauty as well as realism. There is no way to prove this on paper. It can only be proved by speech, by actual production, but that fact is no reason for the assertion not to be made.

I have been emphasizing the tragic value of the play, but it has much comic value also. I do not merely refer to the many laughs which Rice's accurate observation will evoke, but also to the audience's satisfying realization that this observation truly reveals man's state with its faults, foibles, and poignance. *Street Scene* may not have the deft ironies of Chekhov's tragicomedies or the lyrical language of O'Casey's, but Rice's combination of tragedy and comedy, of brutality and compassion, does provide an effect of ineffable poignance at the tragicomic waste of humanity. It is a large play and a great play. The technical brilliance of putting so much together—so much action, so many characters—in a coherent and moving manner, I have scarcely touched upon, but the theme could never have emerged so lucidly and movingly had the play not been so superlatively wrought. *Street Scene* is one of those plays which affirm that the value of drama is that it asserts the value of man. Indeed, the way in which *Street Scene* pushes back the boundaries of the drama may almost itself negate the triumphant brutality of the play's theme. There can be no higher praise, I think, than that.

ii

The Subway was Rice's second play to be staged in New York in 1929, and *See Naples and Die* was his third. *See Naples* was received by the critics with cold tolerance. One critic remarked, madly enough, that if anyone but Rice had written it he would have given it a good notice. Another caustically quipped that Rice had won the Pulitzer Prize on the north side of Forty-eighth Street with *Street Scene* and would lose it on the south side with *See Naples and Die*. The play struggled on for sixty-two performances, and was later weirdly metamorphosed into a movie about sailors that starred Olson and Johnson.

The play is not a serious effort. Rice called it "an extravagant comedy," and, while conscious of its unimportance, was apparently fond of it. In the *Times* for October 5, 1929, he wrote an apologia for it, explaining how its writing was a personal catharsis after a gutting illness and its consequent depression. He said,

> the play, like almost everything else I have ever written, bears a definite relation to my psychological history. . . . The form that the play took was inevitable. It could not be a play of feeling, because I had anesthetized my feelings. It could not be a fantasy because I have not the poetic gift. It had to be what it is: A sort of exotic *jeu de mots*, a sophisticated fairy tale. . . . I enjoyed it enormously. It cured me with its color, its gayety, its extravagance, its verbal acrobatics. . . . a joyous piece of writing.

To me Rice later qualified this statement.

> *See Naples and Die* was not written "lightheartedly" or in
> a "carefree spirit." It was written in a desperate (and
> successful) effort to snap out of a post-operative depres-
> sion, by performing an exercise devoid of emotion or mean-
> ing. . . . The "joy" I experienced came from the release
> that the writing of the play gave me: the knowledge that I
> was able to work. It was entirely therapeutic.[3]

In 1938, when Rice was writing a long view of his career,
he tried to fit the play into a more serious context, and said
of it, "*See Naples and Die* laughed at the autocracy of
Mussolini and at the power politics of Central Europe." [4]
The political satire in the play is little and tangential,
however, and his earlier description of it as an amusing bit
of fluff seems juster. To my mind, the play is a bit heavy for
fluff, however. It has some clever touches in its Noel
Cowardish love story, but it also misses some fine opportunities. One of the potentially best characters, a Mittel-
European dictator called The Beast of the Balkans, is only
allowed to appear briefly on a balcony and does not say a
word before he is shot.

The main trouble with the play is what Rice apparently
liked most about it—"its verbal acrobatics." Here is a
typical passage:

NAN   [*Taking up the half-emptied glass*]   I have a drink.
[*She tastes it and makes a face.*] Boy, what vile stuff.
Italian sarsaparilla. [*She drains the glass.*]

CHARLIE   You want to look out for that. It poisons your
system.

NAN   Listen, dearie, nothing can poison *my* system, any
worse than it is already. I'm so toxic that I blight the
shrubbery as I pass by. [*Suddenly seeing the water-
color.*] Say, do you see what I see.

CHARLIE   [*Adjusting an imaginary monocle*]   Why, yes—
yes, I must confess that I do. [*Imitating* RAWLINSON.]
Coming along rather well, isn't it?

NAN   I can't bear it. My cup is full enough as it is. [*She gets
up and reverses the painting.*] Now, is there any nook

or cosy corner around here, where we can have a nice, quiet little chat?

CHARLIE   You don't like this place? [*Gesticulating.*] Sunny Italy! Lemon-groves and bougainvillea! Sorrento, surnamed La Gentile, the birthplace of Torquato Tasso! The pellucid azure waters of the Mediterranean! Distant Vesuvius, brooding ominously over the peaceful landscape! See Naples and Die! Vedi Napoli e poi—

NAN   Oh, shut up! [*Indicating the chess-players.*] Can't we get away from the ping-pong players?

CHARLIE   Oh, that's all right, Princess, that's all right. They don't know a word of any language you speak—in short, they have no English. Anyhow, what is there to talk about?

NAN   There's a lot to talk about. What do you think I'm here for? Just to pass the time?

CHARLIE   Why, it's a matter I've given practically no thought to, Princess.

NAN   No? Well, then, suppose you sit down—and cut the comedy. And stop calling me Princess.

CHARLIE   Oh, beg pardon, I'm sure. I seem to recall reading in that estimable journal, the Paris edition of the New York Herald—just a moment! [*He produces a clipping from his pocket.*] The very item, I think. [*He reads*]: "Among those seen in the pesage, were Jack Dempsey, the Duchess of York, H. G. Wells, Peggy Hopkins Joyce, Aimee Semple McPherson"—oh no, wait a minute! I'm on the wrong side! That's the Grand Prix at Longchamps.

NAN   Italy hasn't done much for your humor.

CHARLIE   It didn't need much done for it.

NAN   No, just a quick burial.

What Rice is trying for here is the language of high comedy. There is a superb tradition in English drama for such scenes of word-warfare between the clever man and the equally clever woman. One sees it in Shakespeare's rather labored Benedick and Beatrice scenes in *Much Ado About Nothing,* and it reached its highest development in the Restoration drama, most notably in the contracting scene between Congreve's Millamant and Mirabel in *The Way of the World.* Congreve's example is probably the best touchstone, for his best dialogues contain not only the rhetorical forms of wit, but also the intellectual substance of it. His repartee is not only beautifully studded with epigram, pun, and wordplay, but also embodies a significant clash of ideas. Its gayety embodies a distinct moral conflict. He has something important to say.

The lengthy exchange above is a high comedy scene about nothing. The scene has no subject. Nan wants to talk to Charlie, and Charlie presumably doesn't want to talk to Nan. All the rest is decoration. Wit for wit's sake. In such a case, when there is no real subject, the wit takes on an importance that it does not have in Congreve and Shaw. Witty passages in Congreve and Shaw exist to emphasize the sense; this witty passage from Rice exists only for its wit. Consequently, the wit in the Rice passage must be better than the wit which exists to say something. In the Rice passage, we are directed to and focused upon the wit, for there is nothing else to engage us.

Unfortunately, Rice's wit here is not of a particularly rare vintage. It smacks of the quip, the wisecrack, and the gag. Its irony, as in the reference to sarsaparilla and ping-pong, is easily obvious rather than deeply cutting or moderately meaningful. Its satire, as in Charlie's parody of travel literature, is barely distinguishable from the language of real travel literature. Such dialogue needs help from the actors, much more help than the dialogue of *Street Scene, The Subway,* or even *On Trial.* It requires ease, polish, the kind of delivery that brings charm to the words. *See Naples and Die* might possibly have held the stage could it have had virtuoso performances by the Lunts, but on its own merits alone, its inadequacies are too apparent.

iii

The Left Bank produced in October and *Counsellor-at-Law* produced in November of 1931 were Rice's first ventures as a manager, and both did well. Staged in Winthrop Ames' Little Theatre, *The Left Bank* played to three or four hundred people for eight months.

Rice described the notices as "mixed," but Atkinson of the *Times* thought it Rice's best and maturest play, and Nathan called Rice up personally to urge him to keep the play on.

In a 1938 article in the *Times*, Rice described the play as "a story about the expatriates, a study in the psychology of escapism and an affirmation of the belief that one can solve one's problems only by facing them." [5] In *Minority Report*, he elaborated further.

> My new play, appropriately named *The Left Bank*, ex-amined realistically but with a touch of satire, the be-haviour and psychology of a group of American expatriates. Its thesis was that revolt against America's cultural ste-rility was likely to be symptomatic of an inability to adjust to the conditions of American life. In the end, one of the exiles chooses to return to a land where she has roots, rather than to go on attempting assimilation to an alien environment.

Rice's descriptions are accurate. His expatriates are clever and charming, if ultimately feckless and futile, individuals who evade responsibility in time-wasting and pleasure. The main plot centers around two couples—one an expatriate writer and his wife, the other the writer's sister-in-law and her husband from America. At the end, the couples switch partners, and the writer's wife returns with her brother-in-law to America. The highlight of the play is a party scene in which a number of Americans invade the left bank apartment of Claire and her writer-husband, John.

My remarks about *The Left Bank* are made with less assurance than usual, but I think that the play got rather more than the success it deserved. The main plot is a sufficiently engrossing love story, but its patness does not seem handled with enough wit to make it more than momentarily successful, as it is being played. In fact, the paucity of wit and satire hurts the whole play. Story and theme almost demand satire, but Rice gives us nothing so biting. Rather than a sharp puncturing of intellectual pretensions, the play offers only a mild stage humor. Story and theme invite wit, but Rice brings to the play only seriousness.

Rice has been admired by Krutch, Atkinson, and other reviewers for his salty, realistic dialogue. It is precisely such dialogue that the play lacks. Here, for instance, is an excerpt from the lively party scene:

JOE [*Falsetto*] Bye-bye, Lillian.
ALAN I don't think Lillian likes us.
MIRIAM She looks to me like a jeune fille bien élevée.
WILLARD She reminds me a little of my wife.
JOE Don't be nasty, Willard.
DOROTHY You should have more sense, Charlie, than to make cracks about John in front of her.
CHARLIE All right, beautiful; I'll shoot myself through the head.
    [GUS *and* SONYA *suddenly rise and enter* WALDO's *room, closing the door behind them.* CLAIRE, *entering, sees them.*]
MIRIAM We don't like Lillian, Claire.
CLAIRE She doesn't understand la vie de Bohème.
JOE [*With mock gallantry*] Do you like me, fillette?
MIRIAM Go away, peanut.
JOE Embrassez-moi, mon ange! Come live with me and be my love.
MIRIAM Go away, I said.
    [*She pushes him. He falls backwards and turns a somersault.*]

This typical passage moves; it contains at least three stage laughs; it has none of the arch and coy brittleness of the dialogue in *See Naples and Die*; and, finally, it sets precisely the tone that Rice wants, and for these reasons it is sufficiently theatrical. Still, the passage has a thinness about it. It is loose and casual rather than tight and wittily memorable. What the situation requires is an ear like Sinclair Lewis's, and such an ear Rice does not quite have. There is no touch of heightening satire to embed these lines in the mind. In *The Adding Machine* and *The Subway*, Rice had this satiric edge; in later plays he came to write brittle repartee with a more facile hand, but his forte is not wit but the quip. Although this dialogue works on the stage and the play had a good run, one must look elsewhere for a memorable portrait of the expatriate. Hemingway and Fitzgerald did it better, and *The Left Bank* does not seem, to me at least, one of Rice's plays that most cries for revival.

iv

Counsellor-at-Law, one of Rice's most successful plays, was produced and directed by the author early in November, 1931, and with Paul Muni in the main role it ran for 412 performances. Its Chicago company played for twenty weeks, and, when the play was revived in New York in 1942, again with Muni, it had a strong run of 258 performances.

The press was favorable but not enthusiastic, and some of the adverse opinions were rather curious. John Mason Brown spent a "completely fatiguing evening." Nathan, who had delighted in *The Left Bank*, thought this play merely commercial. Atkinson and several other approving reviewers thought the play too long, a remark that Rice interpreted to mean "that they had fifteen minutes less than usual to meet their early deadlines."

The play takes place in the law offices of Simon and Tedesco, and, like *Street Scene*, it has a large cast and a lot of activity. Much of the play is taken up with the presentation of a panorama of character types that ceaselessly flow through the office, and this background is as richly observed as the background of *Street Scene*. Indeed, here Rice dwells more lovingly and fully upon his different social types than he did in *Street Scene*. His cast is twenty-eight, or about a third the number of the earlier play, so he is able to develop his characters more fully. This wealth of detail even gives the central story of George Simon a rich dimension of reality that it would not have if it were played, as it could be, by a cast of half a dozen. Also, because the texture of the play is thicker than that of *Street Scene*, there is less danger of the story being labelled melodrama. Setting the play in a law office causes Rice to lose some of the scenic effectiveness that he had in *Street Scene*, but a law office is an excellent place to bring together many disparate social types. If Rice loses the added dimension that the tenement gave him, he probably gains a greater pleasure of recognition from the audience at seeing his more fully developed characters.

Also, in *Counsellor-at-Law*, the single central story of George Simon is better related to the background than was the story of the Maurrant family in *Street Scene*. There was no logical reason for Rose in the earlier play to take up the central position; the stories of some of the other characters could just as well have been developed. In this play, the attention is necessarily focused upon Simon, the senior partner of the law firm. He is the driving force in the firm, and everyone in the play depends upon him. Even when Simon is offstage—and he does not even appear in the first act—all of the action is focused toward him.

The main story is related to the background in two other ways. The outer office is constantly in a wild flurry of activity—people entering and leaving, telegrams arriving, telephones ringing—and this constant swirl and surge delineates the character of Simon himself. He has caused this activity. It reflects his own character, his ability to juggle a half a dozen concerns at the same moment, his frenetic dynamism. Secondly, in this play Rice is able to divide the main story from the background by a means less arbitrary than getting all of the minor characters, by some pretext or another, off the street. The scene in *Counsellor-at-Law* swings back and forth between the reception room and Simon's private office. For the most part, the background occurs in the reception room and the significant events of the main story in Simon's office. By having two sets, Rice can emphasize his main story and provide a respite from the whirlwind of activity in the outer office.

In this play, Rice found a splendidly effective way of portraying a particular story and of suggesting a whole society. Aside from the excellence of its character drawing, the portrait of society is important to the play because each character has a certain relationship to Simon. The society matron he has married, his snobbish stepchildren, his Jewish mother, his partner, his employees, his secretary who loves him, his clients—all provide different viewpoints of Simon and show different aspects of his character. Toward each, he himself reacts differently, and Rice is able to give us not one or two George Simons but a dozen. We see the infatuated husband, the awkward stepfather, the shrewd and canny lawyer. We see his kindness to the people he knew in his youth, his ruthlessness in business, his exasperation with the young Communist from his old neighborhood who criticizes him for having sold out.

Plays can succeed if they present one facet of an individual convincingly, but the great plays show or suggest more than one facet. In this play Rice has hit upon a device for using his background more dramatically, a device to characterize his hero, and to suggest a full and many-faceted individual. In life, a man is not consistent, but behaves in different ways depending upon whom he is dealing with. Some of these ways are superficial, but all compose the totality of a man. It is a rare play which manages to suggest so many of these ways, and *Counsellor-at-Law* is such a play.

The contradictory facets of Simon's character provide some convincing ironic contrasts, and this extra dimension of irony was not possible in *Street Scene*. Rice once described this play by saying, "*Counsellor-at-Law* touched upon the enslavement of a man of good will by careerism and sexual infatuation." [6] When Rice shows Simon's canny insight at law and his blind infatuation for his worthless wife, we get a persuasive sense of fullness and reality, and are forced also to draw a conclusion about human waste.

The plot develops two main threads—Simon's struggle to keep his wife and his struggle to avoid being disbarred by an enemy who has discovered some shady business in his past. Both stories are engrossing, but an extra tension is added because the audience is aware that if Simon succeeds in either action he will have won nothing of much value. Rice is using Simon as the type of the successful American who furiously chases wealth, prestige, and family, and who, after attaining those goals, is unable to enjoy them because his furious running has become too habitual for him to stand still.

Theatrically, the play has great merits. The whirlwind of activity and the rapidly shifting kaleidoscope of characters give the play a furious impetus. It holds its audience by its excitement. Its minor characters demand fine acting, for much of the effect of the play depends upon them being well etched and playing smoothly together. Although Nathan dismissed this play as being a good example of conventional commercial playmaking, a comparison of the minor characters of *Counsellor-at-Law* with the minor characters of successful commercial plays like *Broadway* or *The Front Page* will show the difference between character conceived as a conventional commercial cartoon and the firm sketch of character that has strong roots in reality.

This play begs for the stage. Without being a master-piece, it is certainly first-rate. It is not as big or as moving as *Street Scene*, but its craftsmanship is often more adroit. Indeed, a play like this, with such a multitude of parts and incidents, cries out for a national repertory company. It has proven its value as entertainment upon the commercial stage. It offers a full, excellently realized, and still valid portrait of American society and the American business-man. It has excellent acting parts. Its language is racy, apt, and fluent. Its effects are many and varied, ranging from humor to pathos to satire. Its pace, the intricacy of its story, the largeness of its cast, and the necessity for first-rate direction put it beyond the resources of most amateur groups. It demands a virtuoso playing of the main part and an ensemble playing among the others that can only be found in a stable and experienced group. Neverthe-less, to perform it rarely is to cast carelessly away a valuable part of the country's theatrical heritage.

v

Black Sheep, written in 1923 but not produced until 1932, is a conventional play with one set and twelve characters. It is a bit dated, but it has a theme worth consideration. It tells the story of the real artist and what happens to him in a bourgeois society, and its theme seems the opposite of that found in Rice's parable of false artists, *The Left Bank*. There Rice seemed to be saying that the artist should not avoid his responsibility to society by running away; here he advocates running away in order for the artist to preserve his integrity. Perhaps the contradiction is more apparent than real, however, for John of *The Left Bank* was really a dilettante and Buddy Porter of *Black Sheep* is a true artist. Neither theme advocates irresponsibility, but different kinds of responsibility.

For almost a decade, Rice tried to interest producers in this play, and finally he had to produce it himself. As he explained the matter in *Minority Report*:

> It seemed time to pay a little attention to my professional life. Since I had no new play ready, I produced an old one, *Black Sheep*, written a good many years previously. I quickly assembled a cast and put the play into rehearsal. But I had lost interest in it; my mind was too much on the state of the world, particularly on the state of America. We opened cold, and though the press was unfavorable there were indications of audience interest. I did not care enough about the play to make a fight for it, so I closed it and immediately set to work writing a new one.

I wish that Rice had made a fight for it. The play is neither masterful nor memorable, but it deserved a better reception, for it certainly was neither awkward nor inept nor, in the final analysis, bad. Rice's early melodramas are no better constructed and considerably less important in their content.

The story resembles that of *Wake Up, Jonathan*. After knocking about the world, Buddy Porter returns to his middle-class, rather Philistine home with his mistress and mentor, Kitty Lloyd. His conventional father, mother, brother, and sister are scandalized and fearful of the effect that Buddy and Kitty will have on the aristocratic Mrs. Abercrombie whose son Milton is about to marry Buddy's sister. The family is about to turn the wanderers out when

Mrs. Abercrombie recognizes Buddy as Tom Hatch, a promising young writer. Impressed, the Porters insist that Buddy and Kitty stay.

The body of the play treats two problems, one embodying the theme and the other the usual stage problem of what boy will get what girl. The theme rises from the story of how Buddy's family and Mrs. Abercrombie attempt to make him over into a socially presentable, conventional success, and Kitty must use all her wiles to pry him loose and pack him off to work. The play also has four love triangles which the arrival of Buddy and Kitty complicates. The love stories require a good deal of intricate plotting that would be more entertaining and seem less complicated on the stage than it would be in the retelling. The love stories are in the play for their entertainment value and so that the serious theme may be swallowed painlessly. Rice handles them with dexterity.

The play contains a good bit of humorous observation and many amusing lines. The dialogue does not have the gauche cleverness of *See Naples and Die*, and there are some neatly wry ironies in it. The background lacks the authenticity of *Counsellor-at-Law* and *Street Scene*, but the stereotyped Suburbia has more stage reality than did the Suburbia of *Close Harmony*. Admittedly, *Black Sheep* is a distinctly minor work and probably does not warrant revival when there are so many excellent plays to revive. Still, it is a craftsmanlike job and could have fared better.

We, the People, produced by Rice early in 1933, had a short, turbulent run of six weeks. Produced in the depression, it seemed forcefully to voice the thoughts of the man on the street. In his autobiography, Rice said that, "The opening night was unlike anything I had ever seen in the theatre. The performance was frequently interrupted by mingled expressions of approval and disapproval. At the end there was a demonstration: cheers and bravos, mainly from the balcony; boos and hisses, mainly from the orchestra." During the run, the balcony was full and enthusiastic, the orchestra slim and silent. Economically, it was impossible to keep the play on long, even though the cast insisted on foregoing its salary. For three weeks, Rice paid his operating expenses from the receipts and turned the rest over to the cast, but it was only a fraction of their salary. Letters poured in urging Rice to keep the play going, and he made a strong fight for it by speeches, articles, and letters to the press. The fight was a losing one, for the theatre would not lower the prices of orchestra seats, and the Broadway audience that usually filled those seats stayed away.

Part of the reason they stayed away was doubtless the critical reaction to the play, which Rice described as "emphatic, agitated, confused and confusing." This reaction seems a classic instance of the theatrical journalist's failure to enlighten. Atkinson's response is typical of the more confused notices. He disliked the play and thought it "a rude, grim, lumbering drama." Yet at the same time he admitted that "the first night audience roared its approval in no equivocal terms," and that he himself was caught up by the play. It is hard to make much sense of this view. Years later, Rice himself described the play as:

> a panoramic presentation of the economic-social situation in America, an exposé of the forces of reaction which stand in the way of a better life for the masses of the American people and a plea for a return to the principles enunciated in the Declaration of Independence and the Constitution.[1]

The play is notable for embodying two of Rice's main preoccupations—the now definitely formed commitment to a drama of social criticism, and what he describes above as "a panoramic presentation." In *We, the People*, he attempted to show many levels of society in America. He attempted to create the illusion of totality that Dos Passos strove for in *Manhattan Transfer* and *U. S. A.* It was the same attempt that novelists like Balzac, Zola, Proust, and Faulkner made in a whole series of detailed novels. Indeed, in two of his own novels, *Imperial City* and *The Show Must Go On*, Rice himself used fiction in this broad manner.

But Rice is primarily a dramatist, and he is important because he several times made the attempt to catch within the limitations of three hours' traffic upon the stage this huge effect of completeness. This attempt to suggest a full portrait is difficult enough in a novel; to suggest it with any success in a play is to challenge most vigorously the traditional form of the drama.

Classic tragedy was concerned with a small segment of society, the ruling class. The Elizabethans broadened the subject matter of the drama to include the engaging specimens of lowlife that we see at Bartholomew Fair or in the Boar's Head tavern. Ibsen drew the drama into a middle-class parlor, and there it has for the most part stayed. Despite the attempts of lively dramatists like O'Neill, O'Casey, and Brecht to pry the drama out of that parlor, the modern realistic drama became almost as confining a strait jacket as had been the form of classic tragedy. For this reason, Rice's experiments with realistic form in *We, the People* and later plays had an importance in preparing audiences to accept experiment. Despite the Theatre of the Absurd, the reigning theatrical convention is still realism, but a freer realism than formerly. It is still faithful in details, but it may cut a few dangerous corners—in its setting or its time scheme, for instance. Plays like *After the Fall, Beckett,* and *A Man for all Seasons,* as well as the simpler experiments of the musical or the bolder experiments of a Brecht, are not now startling to an audience; and plays like Rice's have helped bring about this acceptance. His plays have helped to make realism a tool and not a jail.

We, the People has fifty-six characters and twenty scenes. The scenes range from private homes to public auditoriums, courtrooms, a senate office building, a classroom, a public park, and the office of a university president. Some critics thought too many hares were started in the play, too many themes intruded, too many incompletely developed stories. If one, of course, demands the neat plot of the well-made play, then one will not like *We, the People.* Its many stories sprawl in messy abandon, but each story does have a thematic connection with the others, and from this connection emerges the essential unity of the play.

The various stories show different examples of how poverty affects society: they show the effects of strikes, how one character is forced to give up his education, how another is prevented from marrying, how a typical family is destroyed. Having demonstrated so many effects of the depression, Rice then assigns the guilt to businessmen unscrupulously interested only in making money, to cultural leaders only interested in power and position, and to a small leisure class that exists only for its own pleasure. If Rice spreads his attack, he does not make it unconvincing. He may present specific examples of violations of academic freedom, of racial prejudice, of police brutality, and of the false promises of politicians; but each example proves his central theme that America in the 1930's was a country betrayed by the blind selfishness of its leaders.

Despite its big cast and sprawling plot, the play is not confusing in its presentation or confused in its indictment. The strands of the plot coalesce, and the main characters all become involved in the trial of Allen Davis, which is itself a test case for liberty. The play focuses its attack with increasing intensity as it progresses, but does so without sacrificing its broadness of meaning.

A further criticism of reviewers was that the play did not tie up all its ends neatly. When the play ends, the audience has no solution and no specific political program. It does not even know what will happen to Allen Davis. Indeed, to have written a pat ending would have been to kowtow to the artificial rules of commercial dramatic construction rather than to keep faithful to the strong illusion of actuality which the play up to the ending evokes. Like life, the play presents no pat and ready answers to the ever-present problem of selfish individuals who abrogate freedom. All the play gives is a ringing affirmation of freedom, even of the freedom to fight an entrenched social system. To quote from the long final speech:

> It is of such young lives—Allen's and Mary's and Helen's and a dozen others I could name—that a strong and free people could be built. But what do we do with them? Mr. Williamson has told you: we waste them, squander them, throw them on the scrapheap. The right to live, that is what Mary asks. That is all that any of them asks. And no social system that denies them that right has a claim to a continuance of its existence. In the name of humanity, ladies and gentlemen, in the name of common sense, what is society for, if not to provide for the safety and well-being of the men and women who compose it? "To promote the general welfare and secure the blessings of liberty"— you'll find it there, set forth in the preamble to the Constitution. Does that mean a denial of the rights of assemblage and of free speech? Does that mean millions without employment or the means to provide themselves with food and shelter? We are the people, ladies and gentlemen, we—you and I and everyone of us. It is our house: this

America. Let us cleanse it and put it in order and make it a decent place for decent people to live in!

The theatrical merit of this speech is greater than its literary merit. As theatrical speech rising from the story, it permits the play to end on a note of rousing strength. To descend from this broad and moving statement to a tidy, specific denouement would be to court anticlimax with a vengeance.

The curious strength of the play is that its last scene, composed of several lengthy speeches delivered directly to the audience, is its most dramatic moment. This play would bear revival today. Its artistic merits are many. Its plot is complex, yet clear. Its dialogue, especially in the last scene, allows for stage oratory of a kind rare in realistic drama. Its characters, if not deeply drawn, are not artificial. The college president in particular is a type not previously put upon the stage and unfortunately not developed by anyone else since. The theme may not specifically mirror the problems of the 1960's, but, in some form, the problem of the abrogation of liberty is always with us. In its simplicity of characterization and in its overt appeal, it resembles the better known *Waiting for Lefty* of Clifford Odets. In the broadness of its attack and in the experimentation of its technique, it is, I think, the better play. It has much to tell us yet.

ii

In 1934, Rice acquired the Belasco Theatre and announced a season of three of his own plays, *Judgment Day*, *Between Two Worlds*, and *Not for Children*. He hoped that this season would be the beginning of a permanent, noncommercial repertory theatre. The plays he offered were among the most accomplished and varied that he had written; yet the season itself was the most dismal failure that he ever encountered in the commercial theatre.

Judgment Day, the first play, Rice called "A Melodrama in Three Acts." By melodrama, he meant "tense situations and highly colored incidents," [2] but the term may have been misleading. The play was, as Rice remarked to Atkinson in a private letter, an almost literal transcription of the Reichstag fire trial. As Rice remarked in *Minority Report*:

> Afraid I might have overdone it, I sent the script to my friend Arthur Garfield Hayes, one of an international panel of lawyers who had courageously attended the Leipzig trial. He complimented me upon capturing the atmosphere of a European courtroom and said that, if anything, I had understated the extravagance of the actual proceedings.

In other words, Rice did not mean melodrama in the sense of an exciting entertainment with little serious application to life. This was not the melodrama of *On Trial*, and Rice regarded what he had to say as extremely important. Indeed, as late as 1954, he was quoted in *The New York Times* as saying that *Judgment Day* was his favorite play.

In the largeness of its cast, the strength of its effect, and the pertinence of its theme, *Judgment Day* resembles *We, the People*. It also resembles *We, the People* in its critical reception, its audience reception, and its stage history. The audience reaction, particularly from the balcony, was emphatically favorable. The critical reaction was again blastingly condemnatory. In a refutation of Atkinson's review, Rice wrote to the *Times*, "The cheers of the audiences who are coming to see *Judgment Day* convince me that they are delighted and thrilled to hear a fighting subject discussed in fighting terms." And once more, Rice fought to keep a play on. In this instance, he moved the play to another house, lowered ticket prices, and managed a run of one hundred performances.

The chief charges against the play were that it was unreal, exaggerated, and frenetically propagandistic. These opinions, however, were delivered in late 1934 when the threat of war was scarcely one which Americans wished to face. The country was still in the grip of a depression. There was still much disillusionment about our involvement in the 1914–18 war and an irritation about the nonpayment of war debts. It was more comforting to feel that one could do business with Hitler than to face the prospect of another expeditionary force to make the world safe for democracy.

The closer the play got to the continent of Europe, however, the more pertinent it seemed. When produced a couple of seasons later in England, it was unanimously greeted as one of the best plays of the season, as a just and masterly indictment of a frightening problem. When subsequently announced for production on the continent, the play was thought so pertinent that performances were cancelled in Holland and France and a Norwegian performance was prevented by the rioting of local Nazis. In Germany, the Nazis included Rice's works in a book burning. The unavoidable conclusion is that the play's Broadway failure had little to do with its innate merit and much to do with the imperception of the critics and the temper of the time.

Artistically, the play seems one of Rice's more successful efforts. It has none of the overt preaching of his later *American Landscape* or *A New Life*. The tautness of its plot is never slackened to allow an undramatic discussion of issues. Indeed, Rice was helped in his dramatization of the issues by the form that his story required. That story is the trial of two men and a woman accused of attempting to assassinate a dictator. The trial is a travesty of justice, intended to eliminate some of the dictator's political opponents, but the vestiges of justice still remain, and Rice shows us in Act I, scene 3 the pressures brought to bear upon the one upright judge in the court. In the final scene, the dictator at last appears in the courtroom and is shot by the honest judge who then shoots himself.

Perhaps the quick complications of the final scene suggested the title of melodrama, and the final scene does rise to a concentrated pitch of action. The killing of the dictator is an easier solution than life itself offered and an easier kind of solution than Rice himself offered in *We, the People*. Still, the problems in the two plays were quite different. In a democracy, there is always a hope for a rational solution; under a dictatorship, the time for reason has passed, and violence is probably the only remedy. Dramatically, there are sound reasons for Rice's ending, and one may cite not only stock melodramas that end furiously, but also high tragedies that clutter the last scene with corpses. The only valid charge, then, that might be leveled against Rice's ending is that it is not well done. English critics, however, thought the ending both strong and effective.

A just judgment of this play may certainly now be made, and I think the judgment must be that the play is effective and exciting theatre and that it was a valuable warning that appeared years before its time. It was a gallant attempt to combine with the necessities of the commercial theatre a theme of monumental importance to the nation and the world. The main artistic criticism that might be leveled against the play is that, although it is well done, it should have been better. Granted that Shakespeare or Shaw might have made a better job of it, it seems unfair to condemn an excellent play for not being a work of genius.

Presumably the play could have been better if its characters were more memorable. But, although the play contains no great parts, it does contain some fine acting roles—among them, the temperamental opera singer, Mme. Crevelli, who has a fine comic scene; Sonia Kuman, the fourteen-year-old daughter of the accused woman; Slatarski, the honest judge. These parts are stereotypes, but still they are as theatrically worthy as an actor could desire, unless, of course, he is only interested in playing Hamlet and Cyrano.

In a play of normal running time, an author has two choices. He may try for scope or depth. If he tries for scope, he must have a large cast, and the larger that cast the more difficult it is to cut deeply into each character. If he tries for depth, then he must, as did Ibsen, put only a half a dozen characters on his stage. The plot of *Judgment Day* demanded scope, and that is what Rice gave it. A

Shakespeare can sometimes give us both scope and depth, but Rice is no Shakespeare, and so where, then, does that leave *Judgment Day?* Perhaps where Rice himself placed it—as melodrama. But if we use that term, we must qualify it. The play is a melodrama par excellence, almost a model of what a melodrama can be—that is, a play which engages us with its excitement but also arouses us with its pertinence.

iii

Between Two Worlds was received with even less enthusiasm than *Judgment Day.* As Rice remarked in *Minority Report:*

> *Between Two Worlds,* with a cast of fifty headed by Joseph Schildkraut, came to nothing. It was dismissed with a kind of patronizing condescension that was worse than outright condemnation. The very critics who had deplored the vehemence of *Judgment Day* now took me to task for the mildness of *Between Two Worlds.* With the aid of theatre parties booked in advance, we kept it going for a few weeks; but it was, in every sense, a failure.

Not quite in every sense. No matter with what vapid inanities the critics dismissed this play—it is to my mind one of the most intricately constructed and intellectually satisfying of Rice's career. In dramatic construction, in tone, and in mood, *Between Two Worlds* is quite different from its predecessor; in its own, much more complicated way, it is better. In manner, the play resembles such early works as *Street Scene* and *Counsellor-at-Law,* such later works as *Flight to the West* and *Love among the Ruins.* In such plays, a large group of people is brought together by some arbitrary means: they all live in the same tenement or have business in the same lawyer's office or, as in this case, travel to Europe on the same transatlantic liner. The many disparate characters are chosen for their representative or ideological value. Each embodies a particular point of view, just as did a Jonsonian humor or a character in a medieval morality. Usually, they represent different professions, stations in society, or different social attitudes, and this broad selection of representative types helps to create an illusion of total reality. Each typical individual reacts in his typical way toward the play's theme, and the dramatist is enabled to present a broader range of reactions and a more complexly developed argument than he could with a simple traditional plot.

When each character's reaction to the theme is developed, we have potentially as many plots as we have characters, and these plots are often interwoven in a complex and ironic way. Chekhov, Gorky, O'Casey, and Shaw, in his superb *Heartbreak House*, intertwine their many strands of plot as the strands of a rope are intertwined. Each character is given his due, and no one character takes precedence. Rice, however, in handling this plot simplifies it as do other writers, like William Inge, who are aiming first of all at a Broadway production. Both Rice and Inge make one strand of the plot thicker and more prominent. The other stories are more sketchily handled, and the author thus achieves an illusion of completeness while holding sufficiently to a main plot to engage a conventional audience. Such an alteration probably does not allow the dramatist to gain the splendid ironic effects of the full tragicomic form, but it does allow him to get what he chiefly wants—first an audience, and second a feeling that this is no mere extracted-from-life, artificial, Aristotelian tidying of things, but a full presentation of the sprawling untidiness of life. Such a plot is one way in which some of our most thoughtful dramatists have tried to overcome the simplicity of the stage and to gain some of the feeling of fullness which the novelist enjoys.

The main conflict of *Between Two Worlds* is between the Russian film director, N. N. Kovolev, and the Junior League girl, Margaret Bowen. Rice described Kovolev as "authoritarian" and Margaret as "selfish, anarchistic," and the play as "an attempt to find a common livable ground upon which they could meet." [3] The title refers, then, not only to the ship being between Europe and America, but to the plight of Margaret caught between the Russian Kovolev and a brash, clever, disillusioned American, Edward Maynard. Or, in a broader sense, the title refers to the plight of the intelligent man in the 1930's, who is concerned about the state of the world and who would like to find some reconciliation between the authoritarian communism of Russia and the capitalistic democracy of the United States.

Perhaps Rice hurts the play by reducing an abstract issue of politics or philosophy to the narrow dimensions of a traditional love triangle. This incongruity between theme and story has made many of Rice's plays of social commentary seem inadequate to thoughtful people and dull to theatregoers. However, Rice's method is the only one available for a dramatist, unless he wants to be a closet dramatist. Even that dazzling experimenter Shaw, who also wanted to make the theatre a forum for intelligent discussion, did not break all of the rules of the theatre in a single play. At the basis of that daring experiment *Man and Superman* is a conventional love story, and even that ponderous cycle *Back to Methuselah* is as packed full of laughs as Shaw could make it. The successful experimental dramatist never forgets that his experiments must be performed in a conventional theatre before a hyper-conventional audience. The successful experiments strain against form, they extend form, but they do not finally break it. If the dramatist, as Rice remarked, "writes plays for the theatre, he cannot fail to take the theatre heavily into account; if he writes plays for the library, he is no longer wholly a dramatist." [4]

Using the theatrical tools available to him, Rice wrote as best he could a play that embodied a complex and serious theme. Perhaps if he were a Shakespeare or a Shaw, he could have made the play as popular as *Abie's Irish Rose*, but we might bear in mind that neither *Troilus and Cressida* nor *Getting Married* has been as popular as *Abie's Irish Rose*. Actually, *Between Two Worlds* has great merits as theatre. As an ordered, evocative, and amusing observation of a large group of significant types, the play ranks to my mind with *Street Scene*. If the ship does not quite afford "the brooding presence" of the tenement, the action has a more specific application, and the plot and argument a more satisfying complexity.

Most of the characters are Americans and exemplify the different types that one might expect to find on a voyage of upper- or middle-class tourists to Europe. The characters are also interesting because they implicitly indict the preoccupations of America. The most industrious is Edward Maynard, a successful advertising executive. In a brilliant drinking scene, he tots up himself and the other American tourists in these caustic terms:

> Parasites, that's what we are. Parasites and bloodsuckers. I'll give you an example, if you want one. Look at me. Do you know what I am? An advertising man— one of the biggest in the business. Imagine that. I've got brains, I've got nerve, I can do more work than three average men. I worked my way up from nothing, and what do I make of myself? An advertising man! Next to a stock-broker, practically the lowest form of animal life. What do I do with my brains and my talents? Sell them to the highest bidder—sell them to any robber baron, who made his pile by sweating his hired help and gypping the public. That's how I put in my time. Frightening Bronx stenographers into thinking they smell bad and teasing the wives of Rotarians about the state of their intestines. There's a career for a man with brains. Why a firing-squad is too good for me. A first-class whore, that's what I am.

The other Americans include a life-of-the-party business man with an endless fund of bad jokes, a solitary and rather frightening female drinker, a married wolf, and a woman folk-singer who collects "appropriate native" costumes to sing in. From such a large collection of types, Rice is able to make many effectively meaningful contrasts. Kovolev is paired not only with Margaret, but also with Vivienne Sinclair, a Hollywood actress, and their different attitudes to their profession suggest an essential difference between the two worlds. Kovolev regards the film as a way of saying something significant, while Vivienne typically remarks, "Yeah, well what if she is supposed to be a queen? It's a bedroom scene, isn't it, and I've been playin' bedroom scenes for five years." Vivienne, incidentally, is a fine part, for Rice gives her an intriguing streak of prudery. Another contrast between her and Kovolev is their attitudes toward Vivienne's Negro maid, an educated woman trained to be a librarian and married to a physician. Kovolev treats her with an impersonal consideration, and Vivienne with an indifferent callousness.

Kovolev is also contrasted with Princess Golitzin, a Russian noblewoman whose parents were killed in the revolution and who is now a highly paid beauty consultant in a department store owned by Margaret's father. Although safe and comfortable, she has made people feel that her life has been blighted and that she must be protected. However, the beauty advice that she gives is worthless, and her life is as pointless and unproductive as it would have been had there been no revolution.

A character paired with and similar to the Princess is the American Arthur Lloyd, whose wealthy father killed himself after being exposed as a crooked financier. Lloyd has been as pampered as the Princess. He has received the best of educations and is a poet with a couple of slim volumes to his credit. He is going to Europe to hold down a government sinecure, but he also feels that his life has been blighted and is, like the Princess, an object of sympathy. In these two characters, Rice is making a comment upon the wealthy parasites of two cultures. One wishes that Rice had not made Lloyd impotent. Although impotency fits the meaning of the character, it emphasizes rather than fights against Lloyd's stereotypicalness. Still, with such a large cast and with each character having his thematic purpose, the near-stereotype is as inevitable as it is in the allegory.

A thorough analysis of how Rice pits character against character to make his points about productivity and conspicuous waste would be more detailed than I have space for. Suffice it to say that the play is his most

Chekhovian, and that he has never handled such a large cast with such dexterity and pointedness. Even though his theme is made most strongly by the story of Margaret, Kovolev, and Maynard, it is re-enforced by probably dozens of other examples that rise naturally from the shifting confrontations of diverse characters.

Rice does not oversimplify his theme in this play. His Americans are more than worthless parasites, and Kovolev does not embody every excellence. For much of the play, Kovolev acts like a man with little human compassion, but finally his relationship with Margaret teaches him something about this lack in himself. Both Margaret and Maynard, through the catalyst of Kovolev, change and grow in the course of the play. In other words, Rice has written more than a propaganda tract. If America comes in for more criticism than Russia, America is Rice's own country, and he knows and loves it better. In both cultures, he finds much to admire and much to criticize. His play is an attempt to weld something of the best qualities of both worlds together, and history has made the play even more applicable today than when it was first produced.

As in all good plays, it is difficult to separate the action from the theme for purposes of criticism, but I should note that Rice's observation was never sharper. His eye and ear are beautifully attuned, and he does a first-rate job of the mass reporting that he handled with such effect in *Street Scene* and *Counsellor-at-Law*. The hustle and confusion of the opening is as sharply caught as the opening scenes of the two earlier plays. Rice has a firmer control over his dialogue than he had in *See Naples and Die* and *The Left Bank*. The dialogue here is accurate, evocative, and quite appropriate for characters who exist on different levels of complexity. In the matter of humor, for instance, Rice ranges easily from the inane cheeriness of Henry Ferguson to the brittle repartee of Fred and Rita Dodd.

In sum, there is much excellence in *Between Two Worlds*—the importance of the theme, the rightness and deftness of the complicated plot, the sharply observed speech, the humor, the satire, the portrait of manners. Also, there is little falseness—perhaps only an occasional,

inevitable theatrical simplicity in some of the characterization. The play may lack the theatrically effective murder
that concludes *Street Scene* and the theatrically compelling pace that pervades *Counsellor-at-Law*, but it is a more
intelligent play than either. It is one of Rice's finest
accomplishments, and it may well stand with the great
tragicomedies of Chekhov, Gorky, Shaw, and O'Casey. In
it, Rice did make the theatre a forum for intelligent
discussion; he did triumph over the basic naïveté of the
drama.

iv

Not for Children was to have been the third
presentation of Rice's Belasco season. However, during the
run of *Between Two Worlds*, Rice made a speech at
Columbia University, which contained some astringent
remarks about theatrical reviewers. These comments were
widely reported in the press and brought down upon him a
storm of protest. Partly because of these protests, partly
because of his growing disgust with the commercial stage,
and partly because of sheer physical fatigue,[5] he curtailed
his season and announced his retirement from the stage.

> I have always been, and still am, interested in the drama
> as an art form, a social force and a medium for the ex-
> pression of ideas. I have never been interested in the
> theatre as a place of business or a place of amusement.
> Always I have hated Broadway. To me it has always been
> the cheapest and tawdriest street in the world. . . . the
> theatre game as it is played on Broadway is so pitiably
> adolescent. In the main, it is a trivial pastime devised by
> "grown-up" children for the delectation of the mentally
> and emotionally immature.[6]

Not for Children received its first production the next
year in London and its first American production in 1936
by the Pasadena Playhouse. Rice thought enough of it,
however, to stage it in New York in 1951 under the auspices
of The Playwrights' Company. Then it was fiercely panned
and lasted only seven performances. The chief criticisms
of the play were its confused plot and its archness of dia-

logue. There is no justice to the first criticism, and the second does not seem applicable to most of the play. To criticize *Not for Children* for its confusion of plot seems like criticizing for the same reason *Tristram Shandy*. It is the delight and the excellence of this plot to be hopelessly snarled up. The second criticism has some justice to it, but is scarcely sufficient for a blanket indictment of the play.

The play is actually a satirical tour de force that investigates by discussion and example the necessities, the faults, and the virtues of the theatre. In form, it is a play within a play within a play, and these several compartments overlap in hilarious confusion; even the actors become confused and argue about the matter. No sooner has Rice established a certain convention in the minds of his audience, than he demolishes it. He no sooner establishes that the figures upon the stage are actors speaking lines, than he requires them to speak (seemingly) in their own persons, or he again shifts so that now they are actors portraying actors who are disguised as other characters in a play within a play within a play. There seems no way to make that last sentence clearer.

The play opens with a radio announcer, engagingly named Elijah Silverhammer, who remarks that a play will be performed by Elmer Rice—

> one of our numerous American playwrights. His first play, Street Scene, was awarded the Nobel Prize—[A *Voice offstage:* Pulitzer! Pulitzer!]—Excuse me, the Pulitzer Prize, for 1929, which is remembered as perhaps the most disappointing season in the history of the American theatre.

He then launches into an advertising spiel for a soap powder which has obviated the necessity of bathing. He is followed by Timothy Harris, the producer, whose long introduction deliciously satirizes the ignorance and ineptitude of theatrical producers.

> Maybe I shouldn't be telling tales out of school, but between you and I, when I first read this script, I couldn't make head or tail out of it. I thought it was beautifully written and all that—you know, well con-

structed and everything, but to tell you the honest truth, it just didn't mean a thing to me. I didn't get anywheres. So I says to the author: "Listen, Elmer, you've got a very interesting script there, a fine slice of life I'd call it, but the trouble is it's not a play." Well, of course, he got a little huffy about it. You know authors are inclined to be that way—just a little touchy. Socially, they're as fine a bunch of fellows as you want to meet anywhere—you know, on the golf course or sitting around after the show—but the minute you start picking a little flaw in their plays—ooh!— it's like telling mother that little Willie is cross-eyed. Well, anyhow, what do you suppose Rice's comeback was? He says to me: "What's your definition of a play?" High-brow. As if I didn't know what a play is, after twenty-six years in the business. Well, I read the play again and the more I got to reading it, the more I began to figure that maybe it was one of those flukes that the public goes for every once in a while. You know, like Green Pastures, Journey's End, Grand Hotel, one of those kind. So . . . .

After more in this excellent vein, Harris introduces Professor Ambrose Atwater and Mrs. Theodore Effington, an unfrocked professor and a lady lecturer. They take up positions on either side of the stage to comment on the play, argue about the nature of the drama, and discuss their love life. Ambrose takes the view that the theatre is essentially detestable:

Because it is so essentially false. Because it is so unrelated to reality. Because its emotions are so hollow, its characters so two-dimensional, its speech so hackneyed, its intellectual pretensions so ludicrous, its puppets so mechanical, its philosophy so trite. Because it is the haven of romantics, the paradise of adolescents. Because it is cheap, obvious, vulgar, petty.

And Theodora:

Now I, on the other hand, don't take it seriously at all, and that is why I have such a thoroughly good time. I simply surrender myself to it. I laugh, cry, shudder, thrill—

as I should never think of doing in any situation that touched me vitally. And the sensual stimulation. How I love it. I enjoy the lights, the color, the arrangements of people and things, so pleasing to the eye. Even when the words are stupid, I delight in the trained voices, the cultivated gestures, the graceful bodies, the lovely clothes which I fancy myself wearing.

Then the tableau curtains open, and on the inner stage is played a scene from the play within the play. Clarence, a drama critic, and his wife Irma, a playwright, are having breakfast. The scene is often interrupted by Theodora and Ambrose to explain how the dramatic form limited the playwright. Ambrose aptly dissects it as "frightfully over-simplified" and explains why it must be so. Theodora counters with, "But the essential meaning of a character, its totality—isn't it possible to express that?" Harris intervenes to introduce the actress who played the maid in the breakfast scene, and she sings a novelty tune called "Multiple Personalities." Then the commentators dissect various types of people in the audience and speculate what they are really thinking about. What they are thinking about has nothing to do with the play; nevertheless, this section runs a bit long, and is one place where the charge of archness might be sustained. The satiric condemnation of the nature of the audience is droll, but the point would be sharper if there were five minutes less of it.

There follows the second scene of the play within the play, between Clarence and his mistress Theodora, who is played by Theodora. After it, Ambrose and Theodora discuss the taboos about sex on the stage. Then the tableau curtains open at the wrong time to show two of the cast chatting in their own characters. When the curtain is finally drawn on cue, we see the following pre-Mickey Spillanish bit between Prudence and Hugh:

> HUGH *enters wearing a cap, which he does not remove throughout the scene. Without a word, he strides over to Prudence and slaps her in the face. She takes a vase from the table and hits him over the head with it. He staggers slightly, then recovers.*

HUGH   Well, what have you got to say?

PRUDENCE   [*Throwing the vase on the couch*]   Some day, I'll kill you, you bastard.

HUGH   You won't kill me.

PRUDENCE   No?

HUGH   No.

PRUDENCE   You wait and see.

HUGH   You won't kill me.

PRUDENCE   I killed my dad. Don't forget that.

HUGH   He was yellow, the punk.

PRUDENCE   I killed him. He tried to tell me what to do and I killed him.

HUGH   Shut up, you. [*He punches her in the jaw.*]

PRUDENCE   Bite me. [HUGH *bites her shoulder.*]

PRUDENCE   Do it some more.

HUGH   Shut up, you.

The scene also contains some satire about the attempts of the "starkly realistic" dramatist to infuse poetry into his lines.

PRUDENCE   Kick me. [*He kicks her on the shin.*] I'd like to go out west somewheres. Oklahoma. Where there's prairies and you hear the birds singing in the morning.

HUGH   You got me goofy. I'm nuts about you. [*He hits her in the jaw, knocking her down.*]

There follows then a satiric discussion between Ambrose and Theodora about the pontifical inappropriateness of academic criticism of the drama. Then there is an interruption when an old gentleman in the audience leaves the theatre in disgust because he thinks the play is propaganda. Then follows a scene between Eva, Clarence's and Irma's daughter, and Digby, Eva's boy friend. Theodora and Ambrose discuss this scene and their own problems, decide they are thirsty, and leave Harris and Silverhammer to ring down the first act curtain.

I have related the first act in detail to convey a notion of its complexity, playfulness, and satiric value. From this act, it is apparent that *Not for Children* is a rich play that takes the totality of the commercial theatre as its theme. Its unity is that it is finally a coherent discussion about nearly every facet of its subject. Its specific arrangement depends not upon logical progression but upon surprise, effective contrast, and originality.

The other two acts are as full and in many ways better than the first. There are some amusing scenes at the beginning of Act II in the dressing rooms. We see that the sweet ingenue is a worldly-wise young lady who cleverly repulses Harris' advances. We see Ambrose and Theodora as a husband-wife team squabbling about the play, and Rice has a choice bit when an actress, who is Harris' mistress, comes backstage and cattily compliments them at the same time that she makes them worry about their performances.

Later we get a discussion of theatrical taboos, a tangled discussion among the confused characters trying to unsnarl the plot, an effective satire of the psychological drama in an incest scene, and another scene in which nothing appears but a bed. This scene is followed by an overlong rhapsody from the commentators about everything, from birth to death, that happens in bed. There is another song by Prudence and a final monologue by Eva on top of a mountain where she has run away to find her soul—or something. Her lyrical outburst is wryly counterpointed by her abruptly sitting down and matter-of-factly eating lunch.

Act III presents a cunning parody of journalistic criticism of the drama and some amusing bits indicating what happens when the property man falls asleep. The best part of the act is a play written by Irma—that is, a play within a play within a play. Her play is a rollicking satire that might almost be lifted out of the act and played for itself. It contains every banal, stale dramatic cliché of the commercial theatre.

> Suspense, surprise, mystery, horror, crime and its detection, a touch of the supernatural and the exotic, mistaken identity, an aristocratic milieu, love: licit and illicit, a dash of spice, an unexpected denouement and a neat and satisfactory distribution of rewards and punishments.

It is the most complete collection and the neatest parody of time-honored theatrical claptrap that I can think of.

In the last act, the play within a play is happily concluded, and Ambrose also gets Theodora. Although Rice has often deplored everything in a play being reduced to a simple love story, he seems to suggest here by his conclusion that the pattern is inevitable and perhaps even valid.

Even though I have recounted the plot, I have only touched the surface of its rich detail. For one example, it is a little triumph to name the most charming characters Ambrose Atwater and Mrs. Theodora Effington. According to theatrical tradition, the name Ambrose Atwater has the true ring of pedantic absurdity, and tells one what to expect just as surely as does Zeal-of-the-Land Busy or Sir Lucius O'Trigger. "Mrs. Theodora Effington" has the connotation of the pontifical, stately, and bushel-bosomed dowager who, flourishing her lorgnette, has graced or disgraced innumerable plays. This touch suggests the whole topsy-turvy nature of *Not for Children*. The play is the undramatic made quintessentially dramatic. In it, Rice succeeds in welding the simple and even the zany to the civilized and even the dryly theoretic. It is as fine an example of a play packed with discussion, yet overflowing with entertainment, as one will find outside of Shaw.

Nathan, Atkinson, Wolcott Gibbs, Walter Kerr, and their less eminent colleagues dismissed this play in the most airily patronizing terms. Nathan called it "one of the most irritating of all plays of its particular species." That statement is the crux of the matter, for this play is not one of a species, and any easy dismissal of it in such terms is specious. It may superficially resemble in technique one play by Pirandello, but it is more than *Six Characters in Search of a Play*. Molière, Villiers, Fielding, Sheridan, and Lennox Robinson have all written delightful plays whose theme is a criticism of the drama, but their technique was simpler than Rice's and their range of criticism rarely as wide.

The main faults that I find with the play are perhaps three spots where the speeches of Ambrose and Theodora seem insufficiently witty and a bit mannered. These spots seem minor blemishes, however, on one of Rice's most original plays, a play which I should not hesitate to call one of the most original written by an American dramatist.

v

Despite his announced retirement in 1934, the hope of a repertory theatre impelled Rice to make another try. In the *Times* for May 12, 1935, he explained how a group of theatre people hoped to found such a theatre called Theatre Alliance, and to commence in September at the Belasco with a five play season. Rice had already proselytized for many features of their plan—low admission prices to appeal to a broader than Broadway audience, no featured stars, a series of lectures, a children's theatre, and so on. Elsewhere, Rice explained that repertory has a great advantage over the commercial stage in that, "There are many excellent native plays, written a decade or two ago, which a rising generation has had no opportunity to see, scarcely knows by name. They should be kept alive, must be kept alive, if literacy is a desirable quality in an auditor." [7]

Theatre Alliance failed to materialize because Rice and his colleagues, after months of effort, could raise only $7,000 of the $100,000 they estimated was necessary. However, the thinking behind the idea was partly responsible for the Federal Theatre Project and the form that the project took. Hoping to interest the federal government in Theatre Alliance, Rice went to Washington. Although the government was unwilling to sink money in a private plan, Harry Hopkins requested Rice to submit a plan for a national theatre project. That plan Rice described as his dream of "a theatrical Utopia; a dream that will never be realized, but that I shall always go on dreaming." His long and detailed letter to Hopkins is printed in *The Living Theatre*, and seems a model of what a repertory theatre should be.

Despite the affirmative note of his letter, Rice had

qualms about government interference. At a meeting at the University of Iowa, Hopkins attempted to allay such qualms by stating that the theatre would "be kept free from censorship. What we want is a free, adult, uncensored theatre." [8] Ultimately Rice took the job of New York Regional Director of the project. In an important article in the *Times*, detailing coming activities of the Theatre Project in New York City, he mentioned his own hesitancy.

> I had practically decided to sever entirely my connections with the theatre, with which I have become progressively disenchanted ever since I have been in it. Finally, however, I over-ruled all my own objections and decided to accept —for one reason only! . . . What I saw in the project, what I still see in it, is the first recognition, in this country, that the theatre can be something more than a means of private enterprise: that it is vested with a public interest and can conceivably have importance and significance as a social institution and a cultural force. If this principle can be established and developed then there is some hope for the future of the art of the theatre. Otherwise I see no hope for it, whatever.[9]

All was not smooth sailing, at least for Rice who felt balked at red tape and government interference, and who was finally forced to resign when he protested the censorship of *Ethiopia*, one of *The Living Newspapers*. The Assistant Federal Administrator of the WPA took issue with the portrayal of Mussolini in *Ethiopia*, and set forth the principle that no head of a foreign government should be represented on the stage. Rice thought that this point had been raised to conceal the real issue.

> The dramatist added that the decision to censor *The Living Newspaper* was not made until after he had outlined some of the other productions, including a play dealing with unemployment and the handling of relief and another dealing with conditions in the Southern States.
> "In other words, hitting the Democratic party where it lives," said Mr. Rice.[10]

Protests and mass meetings of theatre people were not able to bring about Rice's reinstatement, and Hallie Flanagan, the project's national director, later wrote, "great as was the loss of Elmer Rice to the Federal Theatre, his protest against censorship was a strong factor in keeping that theatre . . . close to Mr. Hopkins' 'free, uncensored, adult theatre.'" But further: "Enemies made by the Living Newspaper were, I believe, powerful enemies, instrumental in the final closing of the project." [11]

The Federal Theatre Project was a great experiment, certainly the most extensive and perhaps the most interesting ever attempted in the country. Not only was the government taking an active responsibility for the nation's cultural life, but also the organization of the project on a national scale made it possible for a regional theatre to grow independent of Broadway. With the failure of the government to appropriate funds to continue the project, theatre in the United States fell back into its usual rut of imitating Broadway.

Upon Rice the effect of the project's failure was doubtless a depressing proof that his earlier fears had been well founded. However, Rice is a resilient man, and his whole career of endeavor for the theatre might be summed up as a warfare engaged in with small hope of success. Despite the failure of the Federal Theatre, he could still remark,

> there are incorrigible optimists who believe that, given an enlightened administration and a sufficient amount of influential pressure, both from theatre workers and theatre-goers, it might be possible to devise a plan that would provide governmental support for the theatre and at the same time keep political interference at a minimum. Admittedly it is a faint hope; but it will persist as long as there are people who cherish the theatre as an instrument for enlightenment and for emotional and spiritual satisfaction.[12]

AFTER BEING FORCED out of the Federal Theatre Project, Rice spent part of the year traveling around the world and inspecting the theatres of various countries—principally Russia, China, and Japan. He also published a long, panoramic novel about New York called *Imperial City*, and it was not until 1938 that he returned to active production with the newly formed Playwrights' Company.

The Playwrights' Company was a fascinating and significant organization. It was formed in 1937 by Rice, Maxwell Anderson, Robert E. Sherwood, Sidney Howard, and S. N. Behrman as a producing company designed to present the plays of its member dramatists. Despite much initial Broadway headshaking about the company's chances, its first season was triumphant. Rice's *American Landscape* was poorly received, but Sherwood's *Abe Lincoln in Illinois* with Raymond Massey won the Pulitzer Prize, and Anderson and Weill's *Knickerbocker Holiday* with Walter Huston as well as Behrman's *No Time for Comedy* with Katherine Cornell and Laurence Olivier were among the best productions of the year. After this brilliant beginning, the company went on from strength to strength.

The company was formed because each playwright felt, in his experiences with the commercial stage, a disturbing lack of personal growth, of meaningful contact with fellow workers, of continuity, and even of actual achievement. For Rice, the company became the most satisfying experience he had had in the theatre, and he often mentioned the great personal and artistic satisfactions of working with a group of kindred spirits. It is doubtful if Rice could have remained away from the commercial stage, but it is certain that the Playwrights' Company hastened his return and re-invigorated his own interest. In the company's first ten years, Rice wrote and directed five of his own plays for it; he collaborated with Weill and Langston Hughes on a musical version of *Street Scene*, and he directed Sherwood's *Abe Lincoln in Illinois*, Anderson's *Barefoot in Athens*, and Behrman's *The Talley Method*. It was for him a rich, fruitful, and happy period.

In many ways, the group fell short of Rice's ideal theatre, but it was probably as close as a practical man, working in the commercial theatre, was likely to come. Certainly, in some ways the group did attempt to realize some of the qualities of Rice's ideal theatre. One of these ways, of which Rice was surely a moving spirit, was lowering admission prices to attract a wider audience. Their first such attempt, with Sherwood's *Abe Lincoln*, brought more people to the play than had seen it on its original run, but lost the company $15,000. Rice concluded, "as a business operation the venture was a failure, but . . . as an experiment it was a great success."[1] Such ventures, entered into with the expectation of losing money, were remarkable testimony to the company's idealistic concern for the state of the stage.

Perhaps it is pointless to quibble that a company which did so much for American drama did not do more. But, to my mind, the company, splendid though its achievements, was at best a compromise with the commercial stage, and for that reason it carried within it the seeds of its own destruction. As a commercial producing company rather than a repertory theatre, it produced no continuity except for the dramatists themselves. Unlike the Group Theatre, it trained no single body of actors. Although no great company has flourished long without its great writers, no great theatre has ever been born without a standing company of actors working and growing together. A second fault was that the company did not revive its own successes, but concentrated, as did any Broadway production company, on producing new plays each season. A third fault was that it was unable to renew itself by recruiting new writers. One dramatist, Robert Anderson the author of *Tea and Sympathy*, was added, as was one composer, Kurt Weill, and one producer, Roger Stevens. The addition of Stevens was probably the final admission of the group's failure, however, and the acceptance of the methods of every other producing organization in New York City. This changed situation was ruefully noted by Rice in his autobiography.

> Though I still enjoyed my association with the Playwrights' Company, I was uneasy about the changed economic conditions, which made it increasingly difficult to finance plays that did not have an obvious mass appeal, or to keep them running if they did manage to get produced.

Early in the company's career, Sidney Howard died, and later Maxwell Anderson, Sherwood, and Weill died, and Behrman resigned. Finally, with Rice's resignation in the 1950's, the company almost ceased to be a company of playwrights. He was the last of the founding members, and the spirit of the company departed with him.

ii

In the first ten years of the Playwrights' Company, Rice had five new plays produced: *American Landscape, Two on an Island, Flight to the West, A New Life,* and *Dream Girl. Two on an Island* and *Dream Girl* were entertainments, but the others reflected Rice's concern with the issues of the day and were impelled by a vigorous affirmation of freedom. Each of the serious plays proved that Rice had lost none of insight into pertinent contemporary issues, but, when compared to his serious work of the previous decade, each seems written in a lower key of intensity. Although their intentions were just as serious, their themes as strongly felt, and their craftsmanship perhaps as controlled, these plays are looser and less vital than his best earlier work. His eye and ear seemed less

acutely attuned; his experiments were less bold; his scope
was narrower. He had lost the sharp edge of brilliance.

American Landscape opened in December, 1938, and
Rice wrote of it:

> It is, once more, a plea for tolerance, for freedom of the
> mind, of the spirit. It is an affirmation of the American
> tradition of liberty and of the American way of life. It
> is a call to the colors . . . in the sense that the principles
> of our democracy, now in grave danger, are something
> worth defending from extremes without and within. In
> form it is again an experiment—half realistic, half fanci-
> ful.[2]

Although the reviewers for once appreciated Rice's intention, they disliked the play, which lasted only forty-
three performances. Chiefly it was criticized for being too
simple in its statement, for being peopled with stereotypes,
and for using lifeless declamation. The critics were unnec-
essarily ferocious, but there was some justice to their
comments.

The play is set in the living room of the Dale home in
Dalesford, Connecticut. Frank Dale, the head of the
family, is about to sell the small family shoe factory to a
large company which intends to close it down. The Dales
have had their farm home and their factory since the
beginning of the country, and the town to a large extent
depends upon them. In recent years, however, the farm has
fallen into disrepair, and the factory has had a struggle to
avoid being swallowed up by mass production firms. The
father is sick, a son has been killed in the First World War,
and one daughter's marriage is on the rocks. Into this
situation, Rice brings the ghosts of earlier Dales killed in
previous wars, and these ghosts try to persuade the living
Dales to fight for the farm and factory. Two of the ghosts
are women—surprisingly enough, Harriet Beecher Stowe
and Moll Flanders. Presumably, Mrs. Stowe represents a
courageous and outspoken voice for liberty, and Moll a
hardy and indomitable spirit. The two chief strands of the
plot are the family's struggle to save the estate and the
daughter's struggle to win back her screen writer husband

who is attracted by a Hollywood actress. Both plots present a choice between the spurious and glamorous new and the valuable and traditional old.

The title represents Rice's interest in painting as well as the broader intentions of the play. His description of the living room implies that the farmhouse is to suggest America. The decoration "is a hodgepodge of styles and periods . . . a comfortable eclectic collection ranging from the distant English and American past down to the American five and ten cent store. It is not a house of luxury or ostentation, but of good, solid, sensible living."

As the Dale house suggests America's past, the situation suggests America's present. When Frank Dale considers selling the farm to a Nazi Bund and the factory to a large company, the situation mirrors what Rice considered to be a contemporary national problem. On the one hand, was the possibility of selling out to a comfortable isolationism, a *laissez-faire* indifference to Nazi Germany. On the other hand, was the possibility of succumbing to the equally insidious enemy of money-making within.

Despite this solid construction, the play has only a sporadic vitality, and the reason is that the stereotyped characterizations are too thin and the dialogue is too blatantly simple. The living Dales are drawn with some solidity, but the ghosts are extremely ghostly. The ghosts establish certain qualities that Rice wants to stress in the American character, but, when they have done that, they have no dramatic connection to the action. They are a kind of uninteresting chorus. The dull stereotyping is apparent also in the delegation from the Dale factory — Patrick O'Brien, the Reverend Jasper Washington, Abraham Cohen, Nils Karenson, and Henri Dupont. Rice makes his point about the melting pot, but the manner is awfully simple for the adult drama.

The dialogue never rises to the eloquence which the theme demands. Here, for example, is part of the farewell speech spoken in Act III by the ghost of Frank Dale.

> Children, I must leave you now. I must join the other captains who went before me. We've been captains all. Not

generals, sitting far behind and far above the battle; but each a leader of a little band and always in the field. You must not mourn me any longer. There is no reason to mourn. No man should outlive his usefulness. I am the last of my name who will ever inhabit this house. But in you, Connie, in you, Fran, the blood of the Dale family still flows, fused with strange new blood into strong and honest strains. That is the chemistry of America. These few belongings that I knew and loved are yours now. Use them wisely and use them well. In material things, your heritage is a meager one: an old house, a few acres, a little workshop. But man does not live by bread alone. And over and above my worldly goods, I leave you a tradition that is rich and deep and alive: a tradition of freedom and of the common rights of humanity. It's a priceless inheritance. Cherish it! Cherish it! And be prepared to defend it. Do not let the specter of my defeat cast its shadow over you. The past exists only to serve the future, and the future is in your hands.

The speech is better theatrically than in cold print. Spoken with feeling, it could be moving, but it still seems less than true eloquence. It resorts to the trite or nearly trite phrase: "Use them wisely and use them well . . . a priceless heritage . . . specter of defeat casts its shadow . . . not live by bread alone . . . the future is in your hands." It never rises to the phrase that sears itself upon the memory, and seems not far removed from Fourth of July exhortation—true certainly, but not striking fire.

American Landscape was written from deeply felt convictions, and its statement was and still is important. In conception, the play leaves little to be desired, but its execution seems halting—as if Rice were too consciously writing down, having perhaps determined that this play would succeed, that this play would be "for children."

iii

Two on an Island, presented by the Playwrights' Company in January, 1939, ran for ninety-six performances. In an earlier day, its receipts would have been enough for a long run; now, rising production costs and a large cast kept it from making a profit. The play, based on the idea of *The Sidewalks of New York*, Rice described as "a lighthearted comedy." It was written to stave off the depression caused by the outbreak of the war in Europe and by the death of Sidney Howard. A celebration of Manhattan and youth and courage, it exists to entertain and beguile.

The play is another attempt at panoramic structure, and is reminiscent of Rice's novels *Imperial City* and *The Show Must Go On*. Like *Street Scene*, it contains a multitude of incidents and characters although its scenes occur not in one place but all over Manhattan. The first scene starts at the train station and then continues in two simultaneously moving taxis; the second is on a sightseeing bus, the third in a theatrical producer's office, the fourth in a subway, the fifth in Greenwich Village, the seventh in the Metropolitan Museum of Art, the ninth in the head of the Statue of Liberty seen from the outside! These fluidly shifting scenes are one more proof that the realistic playwright is no longer bound by the confines of the front parlor. *Two on an Island*, unhampered by a box set, charms by its free realism. In the original production, the frame of a taxi cab was enough to establish the car, and such mild stylization did not make the show unrealistic. Within the stylized sets, the dialogue and action were so true and typical that they established the reality and evoked a delighted recognition. The play is one more proof that realism is now only as confining as the playwright wants to make it.

The plot is loosely episodic and reveals chiefly the adventures of Mary Ward and John Thompson, who arrive in New York to make their fortunes as an actress and a playwright. After the manner of the picaresque novel, the play reveals their attempts and failures, their meeting, their marriage, their half-success, and their departure to Niagara Falls. Along the way we meet many other characters whose stories become entangled with Mary's and John's. While the minor stories are not related in their fullness, they are quite coherent enough to serve Rice's purpose of revealing a cross section, an essence, of New York.

By far the best character in the play is Lawrence Ormont, the theatrical producer. Like the other characters, Ormont is basically a stereotype, for in him Rice suggests the shallowness, the glibness, the intellectual dishonesty, and the moral poverty that he associates with the commercial stage. Ormont produces what he knows to be trash in order to make money; he tries to bribe the heroine with a part in order to seduce her; he ruins both his home life and his artistic life in order to chase commercial success. However, Ormont, like the most memorable dramatic characters, transcends his stereotype. Having established Ormont as the stereotype of the producer, Rice then plays against the stereotype. He gives Ormont wit, charm, intelligence, and even some compassion. The effect is not to destroy the character's basic stereotypical meaning, but to build upon it and to suggest some of the contradictions and complexities and divided loyalties of a real person.

Ormont is a richly theatrical part because of his arresting breeziness and the fine glib flavor of his dialogue. Rice has lavished good things upon him. When he meets the hero John serving tables in a cafe, he remarks, "So it's you, is it—the Euripides of the Corn Belt! As a matter of fact, I did read the play in a moment of absent-mindedness. As I recall it, it had magnificent potentialities of failure." Or, to clinch the point, here is the beautifully playable section from scene 3, in which John visits Ormont in his office.

JOHN . . . I've come here not only to sell my play, but to learn all I can about the professional theater. The theatrical pickings are pretty lean back where I come from. Now and then we get a road company in Des Moines, but that's about all. And you'd be surprised how many folks out there are theatre-hungry. It seems to me that—

ORMONT [*breaking in*] Some day, when I retire from show business, let's get together and discuss the drama. Meanwhile, if you'll excuse me, I'll go back to casting this little penthouse number I've got in the works now.

Long Island Honeymoon! What a title! What a play! As unnecessary a manuscript as I've ever read.

JOHN   Then why does a great producer like you put it on. Or is that an impertinent question?

ORMONT   I like impertinence. It makes me feel less alone in the world. I'll tell you why I'm putting it on. Because a little exhibitionistic bitch, whose grandfather stole half the country's natural resources, is itching to put on grease paint. Any other questions?—impertinent or pertinent, it doesn't matter which. I'm catholic in my tastes.

JOHN   Yes, I have one very pertinent one. How soon will you read my play?

ORMONT   Can you give me twenty-four hours?

JOHN   Could you read it in a week? I don't want to submit it to anybody else as long as there's a chance of your doing it.

ORMONT   I appreciate that, Thompson. Bernard Shaw could take lessons in manners from you. Tell me, are there any snappy hayloft scenes in this play?

JOHN   Well, there's one situation in it that may be a little hard to get past the Hays organization.

ORMONT   That's encouraging. Next to a good penthouse, give me a good hayloft. I had begun to visualize it as all fine choking dust and the bleaching skeletons of large domestic animals.

To the other characters, Rice gives enough delineation to make their stereotypes easily recognizable, and he makes through them a number of effective satiric and pathetic points. Able actors should be able to flesh these parts out excitingly, but on paper none, with the possible exception of Clifton Ross, the artist, is developed beyond the stereotype. In an earlier draft of this book, I had been much more critical of Rice's constant reliance on the stereotype and of his apparent refusal, except in rare instances, to write three-dimensional parts. He replied:

Of course, you are right about stereotypes, but they are to be found in the greatest plays. (Chekhov may be a debatable exception.) All those unfunny clowns of Shakespeare, those faithless nobles and faithful servants. Also

Molière, Shaw, Sheridan and so on and so on. How can it be otherwise? The playwright has two hours and about 25,000 words to work with. Within those limitations, he must introduce his characters, establish their relationships, engineer their movements and tell a story! How much does that leave for minute dissection of character? If his stereotypes are shrewdly sketched, he provides the audience with the pleasure of recognition, or even identification, which is one of the values of the theatre.[3]

This argument seems to me irrefutable now, although my own training in modern literary criticism made it initially difficult for me either to accept or comprehend it. The real excellence of a good playwright like Rice lies less in his occasional creation of three-dimensional characters like George Simon or perhaps Lawrence Ormont, than it does in his evocative manipulation of stereotypes. An imitative playwright will utilize established stereotypes; an admirable playwright, as Rice almost always is, will utilize established stereotypes with such freshness of detail that his actors can create three-dimensional characters; a more than admirable playwright, as Rice sometimes is, will discover from his observation of society new stereotypes.

In *Two on an Island*, Rice discovers no new stereotypes, no Zeros, no George Simons, no Kovolevs; and we must judge such a play by the excellence of its detail, by its power of evocation. Here, then, is a representative sample from the long monologue of the sight-seeing guide in scene 2:

> Now, folks, on your left is Madison Square. Note the flagpole topped by the Eternal Light and dedicated to the men who made the supreme sacrifice in the First World War. We are now passing through the wholesale clothing district. The streets down here are known as the streets of gold. Look right and left and note the signs. Goldstein—Goldberg—Goldblatt. This is Fourteenth Street. Thirty-five years ago this was the city's Gay White Way. On your left, not far from here, is the headquarters of Tammany Hall, formerly a powerful political organization. Note the sidewalk cafés and restaurants—just like Paris—where tired businessmen

take their secretaries for lunch—with a bottle of wine.
You can get a ham sandwich here for a dollar; with
mustard, a dollar and a quarter. Ah, this is a great city.
We are now passing through Washington Square, a
park immortalized in song, poetry, and story. Once the
home of Mark Twain and many other celebrated writers. Now the Bohemian section begins, the section of
the artists. This section is known as Green Witch Village or, more familiarly to its habitués, as the Village.
Green Witch Village, the gayest, maddest, most unique
spot in New York, where women go hatless and men
wear long hair. [*Suddenly pointing*] There's one right
there on the corner! [*Passengers all turn to look*.] See
the fellow with the long hair? We are now entering
Little Italy, where spaghetti is sold by the yard. Those
white knobs hanging outside the stores are garlic, the
use of which is now forbidden by the rules of civilized
warfare.

This speech is theatrically right; it gets the right tone in
the gags; it uses the right clichés. In the hands of a capable
actor, it should evoke delight and recognition. Still, the
quality of this speech is less than superb. It is immensely
better than Frank Dale's long speech in *American Landscape*, but not nearly as fine as Zero's plea to the jury. The
lines are not so perfectly honed that they bring by
themselves the gasp of recognition; they need help from
the actor. However, most playscripts work in this manner.
The script provides the skeleton upon which the actors
and the director must build. If good performances can
make the bulk of this play vivid, bad performances would
hurt it more than they would hurt *The Adding Machine*.
Still, some parts of *Two on an Island* would create their
own vividness despite the calibre of the performance: the
long and meaty part of Ormont, the pleasure of the
shifting scenes and the set, the originality of the kaleido-
scopic picture, the interest in what will come next, the
pleasure of a deftly handled plot.

iv

Flight to the West of 1940 was one of Rice's
half-successes. In the out-of-town tryout in Princeton,

Einstein came backstage after the performance and told Rice, "If it does not succeed, it is not the fault of the play, but of the public." [4] In New York, the play's press was mixed. The audiences, although slim, were enthusiastic, and the play managed a run of four months. A short-coming of the Playwrights' Company is pointed up by Rice's remark, "In a repertory theatre, or under less rigorous economic conditions, it could have run on indefinitely." [5] The critics who disliked the play thought it merely propaganda, but it was strongly admired by a few others as a serious statement. Atkinson even ranked it with *Street Scene* as Rice's best work. The character of the American businessman who wanted the country to do business with Hitler was generally admired, even by critics who disliked the play, and is a good example of Rice's ability to survey society and discover new and pertinent stereotypes. Although Atkinson's estimate seems exaggerated, *Flight to the West* is a thoughtful and competent example of Rice's plays of contemporary comment. Much of the adverse criticism probably again stemmed from the tenor of the times rather than from the play's own lack of merit. Like *Judgment Day*, *Flight to the West* stated an unpalatable theme at an inopportune time. A prosperous America in the last days of 1940 would have preferred to ignore its "propaganda."

The play again catches people between two worlds. The earlier *Between Two Worlds* had shown a leisurely visit to the cast, to Europe. The passengers aboard the S. S. Farragut had problems, but they had also a bit of time to work those problems out. In *Flight to the West*, Rice portrays a hurried retreat from Europe, and the time has nearly run out. The flight is only a momentary respite, and even it finally requires a decision which is a microcosm of the big decision of isolationism or involvement that Rice implied the country must make.

The passengers aboard Rice's transatlantic clipper are chosen to present his argument and its alternatives. There is a family of refugees who were caught in a bombing and the Jewish Frau Rosenthal whose family fled from Germany and is scattered all over the world. On the other side are Dr. Hermann Walther, a German diplomat stationed in Washington, and Count Paul Vasilich Vronoff, who under cover of teaching at an American university is actually a spy. In the middle are the Americans—Colonel Archibald Gage, who admires Hitler's methods and who believes that what is good for business is good for the world, and Louise Frayne, an American political columnist who is as opposed to Germany as Gage is in favor of it. The three other Americans are the ones who must make a decision and upon whom the plot centers. One is Howard Ingraham who acts as a sort of *raisonneur*. He is a writer whose books have opposed war, but who now feels that the world has so changed that he must question his earlier premises. There are finally the Nathans, Hope and her young husband Charles, an American Jew. Hope is expecting a child, and Mrs. Rosenthal counsels her not to bring it into such a world. Charles feels that he ought to join the army, but hesitates to tell his wife. In more general terms, Hope and Charles must decide upon flight or involvement.

With so many characters, so much necessary exposition and plot, it is impossible in a short space to describe adequately how Rice arranges his scenes. He does it, however, with much craft, with a holding back of crucial elements and with sudden spurts of action for the curtains. For instance, the Act I curtain has Mrs. Rosenthal attacking Walther. Act II ends with the exposure of Vronoff and the decision to land at Bermuda to hand him over to British authorities. The first scene of the last act ends with Mrs. Rosenthal discovering Vronoff's revolver and hiding it in her purse, and the penultimate scene ends with her shooting at Walther and hitting Charles.

Some reviewers criticized the play for being too talky and having too little plot, but the recital of the curtain action indicates that there is considerable plot. At least three stories are developed simultaneously, and that surely should be enough plot to satisfy even the most restless of entertainment seekers. Admittedly, there is much discussion in the play, but it rises naturally from the perplexities of real people in a typical situation. To criticize Rice's dramatization of ideas is really to demand that he have written instead a themeless melodrama.

Actually, Rice has done a great deal in this play to sugarcoat his theme. He has presented well-drawn characters—even the German Walther is no mere goose-stepping Nazi from a Hollywood film, but an interestingly drawn sketch of a frightening type. In the main story of Charles and Hope, Rice has bowed to the desires of his audience. The story is a love story, for the drama apparently insists that its themes be discussed in terms of an individual love story or an individual murder. He makes Charles and Hope young and attractive, rather than middle-aged and fat. Another concession is that the play contains a great many laughs. Like the basically serious Shaw, Rice has tried to entertain his audience as much as possible, without absolutely destroying his basic seriousness.

This argument suggests what Rice has elsewhere implied, that the nature of an audience drags its individual members down to a low common denominator of intelligence. It is true that some members of an audience retain their individual insight, taste, and perception, but these are usually the people who do not like plays. If the theme of *Flight to the West* seemed like talky philosophizing to the many, it probably seemed like bald oversimplification to the few. The intelligent few usually think that a play's simplified statement accurately represents the author's deepest thought upon the matter, and so they leave the theatre to write in little magazines reviews which affirm that the playwright is a boob. Unless a serious dramatist manages a Shavian tour de force—which, of course, Shaw could rarely manage himself—he is under fire from two directions. By the standards of the mass audience, *Flight to the West* was hardly as entertaining as *Hellzapoppin'*. By the standards of the intelligent few, it fell considerably short of a Platonic dialogue. By the only valid standard, of that serious theatrical craftsmanship which falls between pure entertainment and pure thought, the play is not a bad job. It is clear, honest, and workmanlike. It lacks a touch of genius, and it is not a great play, but that lack does not seem a very great flaw.

v

A *New Life* of 1943 ran for seventy performances and perhaps would have closed sooner if people had not been curious about its childbirth scene. In the play Rice's device for collecting his characters is the birth of a child, and the scenes occur in the rooms of a metropolitan hospital. The theme concerns the value of bearing a child in time of war, and the inevitable secondary question of what kind of world one is fighting for the child to live in.

The plot is specifically concerned with how the child shall be brought up. Its mother, Edith, is a nightclub singer who married an army captain who is the son of a rich industrialist. The captain's parents want to take Edith and her child to live with them, and to raise the child to take over a huge financial empire. The wife distrusts her husband's parents, their values, and their kind of life. On her side are some, more or less disreputable friends, particularly Gustave Jenson, an old boy friend now in the Merchant Marine, who is an outspoken liberal and strongly critical of Edith's father-in-law. Gus Jenson and Samuel Cleghorne, the father-in-law, state the ideological contrarities of the play.

Probably the main fault of the play is that Cleghorne and Gus are too tritely stereotypical. The rich man is almost entirely reprehensible, and the poor liberal is almost entirely noble. Further, there is little direct conflict, and the scene in which Gus convinces the captain occurs offstage and is related by exposition.

The play's dialogue is not impressive, and in quality is closer to that of *American Landscape* than to that of *Two on an Island*. Here, for instance, is Gus in scene 8, speaking to Edith:

> Well, anyhow, I did fight in Spain for what I believed in, and I'd be in the Army right now if they hadn't turned me down with this goofy stomach of mine. But what I'm getting at is, we're all in the war more or

less, and that keeps us all pretty busy, but some of us get a feeling sometimes that we'd like to know what it's all about. We've got to beat the living hell out of the Nazis and the Japs. We're all agreed that that's item one on the agenda. Well, after a while, we get that all cleaned up, and then we come to new business. Where do we go from there? Back to where we started from or ahead to something else—something else and something different? And that's where that kid of yours comes in. See what I mean?

This speech is one of several similar long ones, and its faults and virtues are pretty much those of the long speeches in *American Landscape*. It is not rich enough for eloquence, but to overcome its flatness Rice gives it a wisecracking colloquial flavor which is breezy, flip, and fluent. His lowbrow audience must have felt that it was not enough to make the speech interesting, and his highbrow audience that it was too simple to be interesting.

The fourth scene, the delivery of the baby, occasioned some raised eyebrows from male reviewers, many of whom thought it too harrowing or too embarrassing. The scene, however, is done with considerable reticence. Only Edith's head is seen as she lies on the delivery table. Only the voices of the attendants are heard, and a hand occasionally comes out of the darkness. Certainly, the plaint that the scene is too harrowing would hardly have been understood by the authors of *Oedipus Rex* or *King Lear*. Also, the scene is necessary for the play because it establishes more vividly than could any exposition the importance of the child, of its birth, of life itself. And finally, of course, it is a superb scene for an actress. It is rather difficult to appreciate the mentality which unblinkingly countenances in plays a merely prurient sexual stimulation at the same time that it manages to consider this well contrived scene in poor taste.

A New Life, like *American Landscape* and *Flight to the West*, could hardly succeed in the commercial theatre. Its theme was too serious. Once again Rice attempted to coax his audience with story, love interest, and humor to accept his theme, but in this case, even more than in *Flight to the West,* he fell short.

vi

Although Rice's success of the 1945–46 season, *Dream Girl,* was written solely to entertain, it reflects one of his serious preoccupations, psychoanalysis. Although he would return to the subject seriously in his later play *Cue for Passion,* his treatment of it here is purely lighthearted. "I suppose," he wrote, "I never had more fun writing anything." [6]

The play was Rice's last big success, but it was dogged by poor luck. Produced by the Playwrights' Company in December, 1945, it ran for 349 performances, and Rice believed that it could have run another year had not Betty Field, the star, been compelled to withdraw for reasons of health.

The plot is the traditional boy-meets-girl one, but it is lent interest and charm by the play's central device. The heroine, Georgina Allerton, indulges in day dreams which "employed all the clichés and stock situations of treacly romance." [7] The story is constantly interrupted by Georgina's fantasies, and her real life is dominated by her technicolored wish fulfillments. She writes, for instance, a highly romantic and very bad novel, and she moons over her worthless brother-in-law, transforming him into a sort of minor-league Heathcliffe. Into her life, however, comes Clark Redfield, a brash newspaper reporter, whose wise-cracking diagnosis jolts her back into reality and whom she finally marries.

The play is a nice fusion of realism, fantasy, and gentle satire, in which the fantastic elements are not allowed to alienate or confuse the audience. Rice's earlier experiments with expressionism and panoramic plotting came in handy, for this play has a multitude of scenes laid in various places—in Georgina's house, in her bookstore, in a restaurant, a phone booth, a theatre, a night club. Scene changes are handled more easily than they were even in *Two on an Island.* No curtains are required between scenes, but the changes are made economically by raising and lowering the lights in various areas of the stage, and the sets themselves are established by a suggestive minimum. No one would consider *Dream Girl* an experimental or an unrealistic play, and that fact indicates again how the realistic drama has absorbed many experimental devices and become less trapped by its own realistic necessities.

The play is attractive for actors. The central role allows an actress a wide range of styles. Basically she must portray a charming and somewhat naïve young woman, but the dream fantasies allow excursions into travesty, parody, melodrama, sentimental romance, and even a straight reading of Portia's "Quality of mercy" speech. The part is a showpiece for an actress, but a demanding one, for Georgina is onstage 99 per cent of the time. The other actors are not shortchanged. Redfield has many lines of effective flippancy, and all of the supporting actors must play not only their straight roles, but also travestied roles in Georgina's dreams.

Despite these virtues and the play's success, *Dream Girl* is not a major work. It is an entertaining lightweight play, but its fantasy is not inimitable enough to be whimsy and its humor not airy enough to be wit. The point might be clarified by citing the most often mentioned comparison to *Dream Girl*—Thurber's story about Walter Mitty. The device in Thurber's story is the same as that of Rice's play, but Mitty's dreams are more clearly etched and more amusingly memorable than Georgina's. Phrases like "ta-pocketa-pocketa" in Thurber have the hard clarity of being satirically exact and happy. Most of Georgina's fantasies seem softer, fuzzier in outline, even a little off-target. Here, for instance, is a portion of her first fantasy, a radio interview with Dr. Percival, a sort of male Ann Landers:

PERCIVAL'S VOICE A little louder, please, so that we can all hear you. There's nothing to be nervous about.

GEORGINA I'm not nervous. It's just—well, it's just that it's a little hard to discuss your personal problems with several million people listening in.

PERCIVAL'S VOICE I can't help you, unless you—

GEORGINA   I know. Well, you see, I'm in love with a man Jim—

PERCIVAL'S VOICE   No names, please! No one's identity is ever revealed on this program.

GEORGINA   Oh, I'm sorry! I—

PERCIVAL'S VOICE   Go on, please. You are in love with a man named J. And he does not reciprocate your feeling for him, is that it?

GEORGINA   Oh, that's not the point! It's that he—he—

PERCIVAL'S VOICE   Well, what?

GEORGINA   Well, he happens to be my brother-in-law.

PERCIVAL'S VOICE   One moment, please! Do I understand you to say that you are in love with your brother-in-law?

GEORGINA   Yes. Yes, I am. I have been, for years and years.

PERCIVAL'S VOICE   This is really quite an extraordinary case. And, if I understand you correctly, he is not in love with you.

GEORGINA   Well, I used to think he was. And then suddenly he married Miriam and—

PERCIVAL'S VOICE   No names, please!

On paper this passage reads so mildly that it could almost pass for a literal transcription rather than a satiric fantasy. On the stage the effect would be heightened by Percival's tone of voice—a dulcet urbanity that becomes first surprised and then confused. Despite its greater effect on a stage, the satire here is not pointed and precise enough to be superb. Occasionally, Rice's dialogue in the play rises to the genuinely fanciful or the originally witty. For instance, this interchange between Georgina and Clark:

GEORGINA   I happened to have another call. You seem to forget I'm running a business.

CLARK   Running conveys an idea of activity.

But such instances are fairly rare. Clark is supposed to be the witty realist who punctures Georgina's fantasies, yet Rice fails to give him much true wit, and his conversation is most often only flip and glib. It can sometimes rise to the wisecrack, but too often it is just flat. For instance:

CLARK Is Miss Allerton there?

GEORGINA This is she.

CLARK Oh, I didn't recognize your voice. You sound scared
to death.

GEORGINA [*sharply*] Who is this, please?

CLARK Clark Redfield.

GEORGINA [*who knew it all along*] Oh, it's you, is it?
Well, what is it?

CLARK I want to ask you to—

GEORGINA I don't care to hear any apologies. The whole
thing is of no consequence whatever. I was foolish to let
my temper get the better of me. And, as far as I'm concerned, the whole incident is closed.

CLARK Yes, you have got a temper, haven't you? But are
you under the impression that I called up to apologize
for something?

GEORGINA Well, I guess that's foolish too—to expect you
to have the graciousness. Look, I'm quite busy and if you
don't mind—

CLARK I'll bet you haven't done a thing all afternoon.

GEORGINA If you'll excuse me, Mr. Redfield—

This scene, if compared to a witty scene from Shaw or
Wilde, is pretty pale. Rice does not give Georgina enough
of the language of absurdity or Redfield enough of the
language of wit. To convey that she is posing and that he
is seeing through her, the actors would have to do all of
the work by their expressions and tones, for the dialogue
barely helps them. Rice, who has often watched these
scenes in performance, commented after having read my
remarks on them.

> The radio scene plays very well, with Georgina in her
> nightgown, using the bed lamp as a microphone, and Per-
> cival's voice coming tinnily over a loudspeaker. Lots of
> laughs and a good introduction to Georgina's day-dreaming.
> Every line in this telephone scene gets a laugh. In fact,
> the actors have a hard time holding the laughs. The lines
> may not all be comic, but the situation is: Georgina,
> excited by Clark's call and dying to accept his invitation,
> but restrained by her pride; and Clark enjoying her con-
> flict. It is perhaps the turning point of the play; certainly
> one that foreshadows the ending.[8]

The play did amuse many people and it certainly has an immense theatrical potential that does not appear on the page. Still I wonder if it is only a sterile academic quibble to think that it is the play's lack of language which makes it good but keeps it from being superb.

vii

Dream Girl was followed by Rice's last widely admired accomplishment, the musical version of Street Scene, which appeared in January, 1947. For this version, Rice revised and updated the original script, Langston Hughes wrote lyrics for the songs, and Kurt Weill composed the music. The performance according to most reviewers was a thorough success, and even the increasingly sour Nathan applauded enthusiastically. The play was expensive to stage, but it ran for 150 performances and could have run for more had not the producer, because of high operating costs, closed the show in order to cut his losses.

It is outside the scope of this book and entirely outside my competence to discuss its artistic merits as folk opera. The consensus of more learned men was that it was an accomplishment worthy to rank with Porgy and Bess. That is high praise, indeed.

7   THE LOSER

RICE'S LAST PLAYS produced in New York were *The Grand Tour* of 1951, *The Winner* of 1954, and *Cue for Passion* of 1958. None was enthusiastically received by either critics or public. The first ran for eight performances, the second for thirty, and the last for thirty-nine. Nevertheless, these plays were not the poor failures that reviewers' comments or box office results implied. In most reviews, critics discussed the story and the characters, but missed the theme. Rice's themes were not obscure, in the sense that Beckett or Ionesco might be thought obscure. Indeed, with his unerring instinct for crucial issues, he had picked themes of much pertinence for America in the 1950's. In the broadest sense, the plays are about selflessness and selfishness. *The Grand Tour* and *The Winner* are about the relation of morality to money, and *Cue for Passion* is a psychoanalytic retelling of the Hamlet story that shows what would have happened had the characters acted according to reason rather than to passion. Such themes had perhaps so much relevance that their points were hard to see. At any rate, when the themes are seen, the value of the plays themselves appears considerably enhanced.

i

The Grand Tour opened in December, 1951, to imperceptive notices. A few reviewers were moved by the freshness and charm of the last scene of the first act, but most missed the point of the second act, and condemned the play for not living up to its expectations. Typical of this view was Walter Kerr's summing up of the play as a "genial excursion into small talk." This remark seems so totally wrong that one hardly knows how to reply to it. Rice could scarcely have hit upon an issue more relevant to contemporary America than the relationship of morality to money. In modern America, there is apparently a dual morality about money: the modern view that money is the root of all happiness, and the traditional view that it, if not the root of all evil, as at least not essential to the good.

These two views are represented in the play by the hero and the heroine. The hero, Ray Brinton, is a banker whose marriage and career have gone on the rocks. He calls himself with telling accuracy "a victim of prosperity." He lived beyond his income not because he was keeping up with the Joneses, but because "we were the Joneses!" To cover his losses, he speculated, lost, took money from the bank in order to recoup, and got ever deeper in debt. His story is quite usual, and his reaction to it even more usual.

> I feel no particular guilt about the money part of it. Nobody's hurt, except my bonding company, and the loss means nothing to them. Besides, lots of respectable people got their money in ways that aren't so different: evading taxes, bribing public officials, engineering shady deals, driving weaker competitors to the wall, prostituting their talents. The world is rotten with all kinds of corruption that's a lot more immoral and degrading than just plain theft. I'm not justifying what I did, but I'm not horrified by it, either.

The reviewers pounced upon this story as too tritely typical, but it is really prototypical. Its usualness is its strength. Ray's view is so widely accepted that the theme of the play is cuttingly pertinent. Consider a play with a similar theme from an earlier time—say, Lillo's *The London Merchant*—and notice with what horror all of the characters regard the malefactor. In Rice's play, everyone excuses the culprit, minimizes the importance of his crime, and tries to cover it up. The casualness with which Ray's crime was accepted by Rice's characters seems to have carried over to the reviewers, for they too failed to be horrified by his plausibly sounding apologia.

The traditional moral view is presented by the heroine, Nell Valentine, an aging but engaging and still attractive school teacher. She has come into some money from her father's insurance, but she has earned that money by scrimping and sacrifice, and now finally she is having a fling, taking her Grand Tour. On the boat, she meets Ray, learns how his marriage has become more and more pointless until his wife has now gone to Reno, and finally she falls in love with him. When he tells her of his embezzlement, she tries to persuade him to accept her money to pay off the bank. He refuses. However, an official of the bank arrives, and so shortly does Ray's former wife. When Nell sees that the wife still loves him, she gives her money to the bank official and leaves. In the final scene, we see her teaching school in the Fall and telling her class of her summer's "grand" tour.

These bare bones of the story sound like formula fiction, but any story, reduced to its skeleton, is shopworn, and the value of a story is really determined by the author's ability to invest it with engaging detail. In the specific details of her character, Nell is well portrayed. She is not the stereotyped, pitiably-plaintive schoolmarm taken in by the city slicker, but an intelligent, warm, and appealing type who convinces the audience of her importance. The chief reason for that importance is that she is, quite simply, a moral person to whom money is a boon, but not the main reason for existence. She gives that money up to a man who has come by his own money with much less labor, a man to whom money does not even represent as much happiness as it does to her. Money did not save Ray's marriage from becoming meaningless, but money will enrich Nell's life. Like the important characters in Rice's other recent plays, Nell acts selflessly. Boiled down to its simplest statement, selflessness is the basic lesson of Rice's recent work.

There is sentiment in the play, and the heroine has

renounced love in the time-honored manner of the heroine of romance. Yet Rice handles her renunciation plausibly. Nell hides her feelings. She wards off sentiment by gayety and even by jokes, and the emotion of the play is consistently understated. Nell has no *grande dame* scene of renunciation, nor does the play end with her expiring in consumption or dying of a broken heart. It ends with her giving a matter-of-fact lecture to her students, and this excellent ending only hints at her emotion. This underplaying generates a fine theatrical tension between what she says and what the audience knows she feels. It works better than an easy tearing passion to tatters.

One final point about Nell. The play is hers, and she is so fully caught that one might think of *The Grand Tour* as a vehicle play—indeed, Rice originally intended the part for Helen Hayes who was, because of her husband's illness, unable to play it. Without pulling out all of the emotional stops, Rice has given Nell a wide range of emotions, and this is merely another way of saying that she is, if not vitally memorable, a very full type. This is the kind of part that the great actresses of the nineteenth century would have kept in their repertoires for years.

The last scene of Act I is one of the most effective scenes that Rice has written in recent years, and it indicates how unobtrusively and well he has woven experimentation into the fabric of realism. Here is how he sets the scene:

> Paris. The stage is bare. In the background is a sky drop upon which is painted a stylized version of the Arc de Triomphe or some other familiar Paris landmark. Throughout the scene, an off-stage piano plays traditional and popular airs appropriate to the mood and movements of the characters, and the light varies with the changing locales and the time of day. A moment after the rise of the curtain, NELL and RAY enter. He carries a guidebook, she a camera, which she uses occasionally. During the scene, they move continually back and forth across stage. Their speech and behavior are slightly stylized. As indicated in text, much of what

NELL says represents her thoughts and is not heard by RAY.

Rice takes the two on a tour of Paris: from the Eiffel Tower to the The Invalides to the Place de la Concorde to the Louvre where they see the Venus de Milo and the Mona Lisa, to a hat shop, to the Cafe de la Paix, to Maxim's, to the Folies Bergeres, to a night spot in Montmarte called The Dead Rat, and finally, as the sun comes up, back home. With just off-stage music and stage lighting and the abilities of two actors, Rice manages to create the city, and he does it not through any brilliantly startling stage gimmicks, but through a purely realistic and theatrical stage dialogue that creates its own verve and zest. The scene really testifies to what lengths theatricality can enliven realism. It reminds one of the flying scene in *Peter Pan* or the apotheosis of Dublin in the third act of O'Casey's *Red Roses for Me*.

There is nothing in the second act so spectacularly fine, but there is enough plot to engross an audience and to prevent it from feeling let down. With such virtues, the rejection of *The Grand Tour* by the commercial critics seems a gross misreading. In theme it is highly relevant; in manner, it is able to work expressionism and sentiment into a basically realistic play, without alienating its audience by the combination; in characterization, it is full; and in detail, it is charming. It is not a great play, but it is a meaningful and accomplished one.

ii

The Winner also has a theme concerning morality and money, embodied in a story whose main character is a woman. Once again, the critics failed to see the theme, and thought the play only an ambling and amiable Cinderella story aimed at the commercial market. The central problem of the play is whether one should adopt an attitude of morality or of expediency toward the accumulation of money. The play's heroine runs against the grain of the times by valuing the moral credit above what is in this instance the immoral cash.

The story is complicated to relate, but clear enough upon the stage. An elderly businessman with a bad heart proposes that the heroine Eva Harold live with him in Cuba, and tells her that he has made out a new will in her favor. The heroine is poor, and so is the man she wants to marry, David Browning, a young lawyer. The lawyer is himself married, but "everytime he and his wife get all set for a divorce, something else happens." The businessman, Arnold Mahler, dies in Eva's apartment of a heart attack, as his wife and a private detective burst in.

The remaining scenes depict two problems: the court fight which Mrs. Mahler instigates to contest the will, and Eva's own conflict about whether to fight for the money. Representing Mrs. Mahler is Martin Carew, a rich and successful lawyer, and representing Eva is David. Carew tries to buy Eva off, and she refuses, although puzzled about whether she is entitled to anything. David counters with, "Look, you don't have to convince me of the importance of moral issues. It's something we all have to face, all the time, in the kind of world we live in." But in the same speech, he finally decides, "Everybody has to make some compromises, and it's a question of weighing one set of values against another. In this case, it might be our whole future against a pretty abstract principle." In other words, for reasons of expediency, he thinks she should allow herself to be bought off.

Eva decides, however, to fight, mainly in order to "show those smart reporters and those tabloid readers that I'm not a gold-digging tart, who tried to tease a half-crazy old man out of his money." She tears up Carew's check, even though she is almost certain that she will lose the case, and the second scene closes with wry effectiveness as, "Munching the apple she goes to the center table, sees the torn check, mourns ruefully and begins putting the fragments together."

The third scene is a private hearing in the judge's chambers—a Negro judge, incidentally—and culminates with the judge urging a settlement "before there are new disclosures of base passions and ignoble motives." Eva refuses to quit because, "if I let them buy me off, why it's like some kind of racket—blackmail, if that's what you call it—and I don't see how I could ever be happy about it." In other words, though wanting the money desperately and though fairly certain that by continuing to fight she will lose it all, Eva still puts a principle before the money.

In the final scene in Eva's apartment, we learn that she has won, and she is delighted that the judge has morally vindicated her. She thinks momentarily that she can have her cake and eat it, but David explains that there is the threat of an appeal which Mrs. Mahler will waive if Eva will split the estate. David advises compromise. Carew, who is now out of the case, appears with some news that David had concealed. Mahler had owed a great deal of delinquent taxes, and, if Eva refuses compromise, Mrs. Mahler will inform the government. Carew points out that Eva's reasons for buying Mrs. Mahler off would speciously negate her previous honest reasons for fighting. Without tying the plot up precisely, Rice clearly indicates that Eva will refuse to compromise and will therefore lose all of the money to the government. As the curtain falls, Carew is trying to explain the case and his own interest in Eva to her mother over the telephone, and he and Eva are preparing to go out to dinner.

This summary has not made all of the facets of the plot clear, but perhaps enough is here to indicate that the squabble about money is, as are most such squabbles, both complex and dirty. The general opposition of morality versus expediency is, however, quite clear. Today, morality often becomes confused with expediency, no matter whether the issue is money, position, or international politics. The arguments in favor of expediency are so lucidly, frequently, and cogently put that there is difficulty even for the perceptive man of good will to untangle the specious reasoning from the valid. The fable of Eva and the will is an apt example of this difficulty and an answer to it.

The characterization offers considerable scope for actors. The heroine's part is full and vivid, and Carew is one of

Rice's best worldly wise men. Some critics found the dialogue awkward or, in the case of the judge's moving and restrained plea, stilted and banal. To me, the dialogue seems for the most part supple and fluent, and many of Carew's lines have a nice wit. For instance:

EVA   David and I have been talking about getting married for two years.

MARTIN   No conversation can be successfully sustained that long.

The importance of the theme, the absorbing nature of the story, the well-drawn characters, and the more than adequate dialogue make *The Winner* one of Rice's best-wrought plays. The problem at the heart of the play shows Rice once again acting as the "mirror of his times" and "the weathervane of the popular climate." Rice is more than a recorder, however; he is also a conscience, and his latest plays stress the necessity of behaving well. The more currently popular playwrights have been cannier; they have written about the pleasures of behaving badly.

iii

Cue for Passion, Rice's most recent Broadway play, appeared in November, 1958, and had a short run of thirty-nine performances. It might have run longer had a newspaper strike not made it impossible to advertise the play properly. Its reception by the reviewers, however, would scarcely have helped its run, for they greeted it with lukewarm approval to which were attached many reservations. In *Minority Report*, Rice remarked that the theme of the play,

> derived from an essay by the English psychoanalyst Ernest Jones in which he suggests that Hamlet's inaction was due neither to infirmity of will nor to doubt about the guilt of Claudius, but to his self-identification with the murderer, who had actually realized Hamlet's Oedipean wish to kill his father and marry his mother. In other words, it was Hamlet's unconscious feeling of shared guilt that kept him from vengeance.
>
> In a modern California setting, I developed a play upon

this thesis. I did not, as some commentators suggested, attempt to "rewrite" *Hamlet*; I could hardly have been so fatuous as that. I merely took the central situation of *Hamlet* and tried to examine it in the light of modern psychology. The play had a "happy" ending, in the sense that the young protagonist comes to an understanding of his fixation and is thus enabled to shake off his bondage to his mother. The play's title, *Cue for Passion*, was taken from one of Hamlet's soliloquies.

The hero, Tony Burgess, is a young man suffering from that popular malady the Oedipus Complex. For four of the play's five scenes, this fact makes him an effective character, and it also raises the plot to an absorbing pitch. When in scene 4, Tony becomes more and more drunk until he whips out a pistol to fire through the window at the figure whom he thinks is his stepfather, the play has been brought to its tensest and most theatrical moment. Up to that point, Rice had built his play and involved his audience beautifully.

The influence of psychiatry upon the final scene, however, extracts much of the drama from what up to then had been a compelling experience. The pattern of modern psychiatry is not awfully different from the classical definition of tragedy—fault, suffering, catharsis, and healing. If we accept Aristotle's analysis of the function of the drama, we may well believe that the drama and psychiatry attempt are, more or less, the same thing. For that reason it might seem that the two could be effectively welded together. That they cannot is, I think, proven by this play.

Psychiatry must cure by overt statement, but the drama depends upon implicit statement for its major effect. Psychiatry must cure by making a patient clearly aware of what is at the bottom of his disturbance. With this awareness, the patient will, presumably, be able to overcome his problem. In this play, the growth of awareness comes in the final scene when Tony's friend Lloyd discusses his problem with him in approved psychiatric fashion. When Tony understands, he then attempts to cope with his problem by leaving his mother, and he will then, it is implied, be able to work his way back to normalcy.

Psychiatrists will be unhappy with the play, for Tony's growth of awareness must by dramatic necessity come faster and more easily than it might in life. But if we allow that the play embodies as sufficiently plausible an example of the psychoanalytic pattern as the drama allows, we must yet face the problem of what effect this pattern has upon *Cue for Passion* as a piece of theatre. To my mind, the effect is deadly. It prevents the story from rising to a traditional theatrical climax and substitutes an untheatrical false climax. The conclusion of the psychiatric pattern must be the cure which can only come from overt statement by the therapist and understanding by the hero. To attain understanding, the hero must be calm and self-possessed. For four scenes, Rice has made Tony more and more driven, more and more rawly exacerbated, but instead of pushing him to the final, logical, theatrical pitch of exacerbation by the murder of his stepfather, a la Shakespeare, Rice has the wounding of the Polonius figure snap Tony out of his hysteria. In the last act, Tony is lucid, thoughtful, reasonable, remorseful, and controlled. He is determined to cure himself and leave his mother before he brings about a catastrophe. It may be psychologically plausible that the wounding of Dr. Gessler was enough of a shock to bring Tony back to his senses, but it is also dramatically unhappy. Playgoers, rightly or wrongly, have been conditioned to demand the height of intensity to appear at the end of a well-constructed plot; here Rice denies that satisfaction, and people came away from the play feeling somehow cheated. The audience in this instance demanded the traditional form of tragedy, but Rice, like Shaw in such plays as *Back to Methuselah*, was determined to go beyond tragedy and give the audience something less barbaric and more civilized. However, the dramatic form is not civilized enough to survive reason, in the form of the psychiatric pattern, and to avoid the bloody Shakespearean climax is to court disaster. Tragedy barbarically attempts to present the entirety of the tragic action, including the gory climax, and that tragic pattern is what audiences expect and desire—the satisfaction of vicarious blood-spilling and not the thin, unemotional rewards of learning and understanding.

The many critics who condemned this play for not being as good as *Hamlet* were largely unconcerned with the pattern of tragedy and criticized Rice at his most unassailable point, the texture of the play. Some criticized the play for not following the story closely; yet the parallels are sufficient for us to recognize the prototypical story, as indeed the parallels of the Hamlet story with the Orestes story were clearly enough there for any Elizabethan with sufficient wit to recognize them. There is no point by point identity, for Rice was not attempting a Joycean tour de force. We have the same situation, but not the same treatment. Rice gives us a rich character in his Hamlet, a Gertrude, a Claudius, a fine Polonius, an Ophelia, and a friend of Hamlet who is something of Horatio and something of Rosencrantz and Guildenstern. He even manages a realistically acceptable ghost scene in Tony's drunken hallucination, but there the parallel stops. Rice is not trying to rival Shakespeare, any more than Shakespeare was trying to rival Froissart or Plutarch or Boccaccio or Hollinshed. No modern critics have condemned Anouilh because his individual *Antigone* was not as fine as Sophocles's or his particular version of Joan of Arc not as fine as Shaw's. Anouilh's characters are his own, and so are Rice's. Further, to criticize Rice for not having written language as great as Shakespeare's is to criticize him, in the first place, for daring not to wreck his play and, in the second place, for impudently presuming not to be a genius.

Having said that the basic fault of *Cue for Passion* lies in its use of the psychiatric pattern, one must add that the play offers some strong acting roles, a fine soliloquy, and, through most of its length, a tense plot. It is also one of the most nearly successful experiments in recent years in wrenching the realistic drama away from its traditional naïveté. Like *The Grand Tour* and *The Winner*, it probably fails in its attempt to lift its audience, but what an honorable failure it is.

Love among the Ruins is not one of Rice's best plays, but I will treat it in detail because it is the only one that I have directed and because I had the benefit of Rice's advice during the last week of rehearsal. Largely, the story of the production is the story of my own confusion, but some of Rice intentions as author and something of his practice as a director ultimately seep through the fog of my misapprehensions. From the story of the production also emerge some basic faults of college dramatics, and for these reasons I shall sketch in a bit of background.

I was a visiting professor of English and an adviser for student dramatics at a small, rich university in upstate New York, for the school year of 1962–63. The university, although it had a well-known and highly endowed school of music, had no department of dramatics and offered no courses in practical theatre. Campus productions were organized largely by three or four different student clubs. For the first semester, I succeeded in merging most of these groups to produce an Irish drama festival of five plays, including the world première of an O'Casey, the American première of a Paul Vincent Carroll, and two lectures on the Irish drama by Padraic Colum and Denis Johnston. On the second night of Colum's experimental play *Moytura* and Johnston's powerful study of Swift *The Dreaming Dust*, only eighty people came into an auditorium that seated 1100, and in the afternoon only thirty people attended Johnston's excellent lecture. The reception of the plays by the local press was unenthusiastic and by the campus press savage. The plays were described as "of dubious merit" and the performances as "execrable." The distinguished Padraic Colum was labelled an "esoteric poetaster," and Johnston's fine play called "a frumpy, jumpy, weepy, sleepy concatenation of bad last scenes from every bad play you have ever seen." Carroll's *The Devil Came from Dublin* was filled with "stock characters out of some dusty book on How to Write a TV play," while O'Casey's *Behind the Green Curtains* was "a tendentious bore, an unhappy melodrama." All in all, the reviewers had "a feeling of dismay and insult."

The effect of this bombardment on students who had gone through six arduous weeks of rehearsals with élan and vigor was to knock all of the spirit and fight out of them. Despite my assurances that they had done nobly and well, they relapsed the second semester into their separate clubs and planned a conventional group of plays. My own notion of a college theatre is that it should not rely solely or even primarily upon the production of classics or currently admired commercial productions, for all of the dead college theatres in the country do that. If there is any place to create a living repertory, any place to fight against the slavish imitation of the commercial stage, any place to allow both established and new writers to have performed plays that the commercial stage would not do, a college theatre seems most definitely it.

Consequently, I wrote letters of inquiry to various established writers, asking for any old or new plays which the commercial stage was unlikely to produce. One heartening reply came from Rice, who said that he had no new play available, but that he had one written about ten years before, called *Love among the Ruins*. The play had never been produced, "whether," he said, "because it does not merit production, or because it is not 'commercial,' I don't know."

The play turned out to be in two acts and took place in the Roman ruins of Baalbek in Lebanon, in 1950. The main characters were Arthur Dewing, the elderly head of an archaeological expedition, and Suzanne, his young wife. As the play opens, we see that Dewing's young assistant, Carl Hannay, has an awkward boyish crush on Suzanne, and that the Dewings don't know exactly what to do about it. A party of American tourists arrives, consisting of an Anglican bishop, his wife, his daughter, a fussy middle-aged school teacher, a successful oil promoter, and Neil Davis, Suzanne's first husband. Davis has come to win Suzanne back. He had divorced her during the war, but the fault Rice largely lays upon the disruption of the times. Davis is now a worthwhile and promising man who offers Suzanne an exciting future as well as the children which Dewing cannot give her.

Suzanne's choice is not easy. Although she loves Davis and fervently wants children, she also loves and respects her husband. We have here a typical Ricean triangle of two men and a woman, with one of the men considerably older than the other. The same triangle appears in *Two on an Island*, *The Winner*, *Cue for Passion*, and in Rice's novel *The Show Must Go On*. In these other instances, the older man had been wiser or at least more worldly wise, more glib. Here, the glibness is played down and the wisdom emphasized. Dewing is rather a model of what Rice expects from a civilized man—integrity, compassion, concern for others, and a tight rein on his passions.

Carl, Davis, and Dewing exhibit three varieties of love: Carl, the infatuation of a young man unable to disguise or restrain his feelings; Davis, the healthly physical need which is, nevertheless, more controlled and maturely motivated than Carl's puppy love; and Dewing, the mature love of an experienced man who can put the other person first and who can restrain his emotions no matter how deep they are. The other characters also exhibit varieties of love. Bishop Bicknell shows how a love of God has become thwarted by ambition. His callous daughter, Florence, has "been shot out from under three husbands." Clinton Grue, the businessman, is a mere sexual opportunist. Laura Hardwicke, the school teacher, is a spinster who mourns a chance she lost in her youth and who now feels full of regret and loneliness.

Rice wants to show how these varieties of love are equipped to deal with the postwar world and perhaps how they have helped bring that world about. Of these varieties, Dewing's love comes closest to selflessness. He makes no emotional demands upon Suzanne as Davis does. Despite the pressure of private agony, he allows her to make her own decision. The others all act with degrees of selfishness both in their personal and their public lives.

If the basic problem of the play is how to react to the ruins of the postwar world, and the primary answer is by a compassionate and civilized selflessness, there are also other alternatives advanced. The bishop is the spokesman for a church which has become ineffectual; Grue is the spokesman for a commercial world which is ruthless, selfish, and opportunistic; the character of Florence suggests ignoring the problem completely and simply drifting.

As in so many of Rice's plays, the problem is defined by a decision which the heroine has to make about her personal life. Suzanne's problem might be taken as an example of how to react to the postwar world. The general theme is also presented by overt discussion and suggested by the effective setting of the ruins of Baalbek. In the description of the set, Rice remarks, "The whole effect is one of hopeless desolation and inexpressible grandeur." As the play progresses, it becomes increasingly clear, without ever intrusively explicit, that the ruins may well be taken as the ruins of the postwar world itself.

To me, the play appeared thoughtful, well-structured, with an absorbing story line, an important theme and, for the most part, well-etched characters. The drawbacks I thought fairly minor, and later, after talking to Rice, I was sure they were irremediable. First, there was no real ferocity or strong drama about the play; save for a scuffle in the last act it was in a muted minor key. The language seemed fluent, but hardly vivid or distinguished. Much of the talk in the second scene seemed only talk, lacking the fire and clash of ideas that one might expect in a similar scene by Shaw. The curtains were nicely theatrical, but I thought the entrances in the third scene a bit contrived. The main character, Dewing, was a fine and full one, and Suzanne was another of Rice's convincing gallery of women. The rest seemed merely theatrical types, and the businessman a somewhat overdrawn one. It seemed a play which might be quietly satisfying, but hardly exciting.

Feeling such a comparative lack of enthusiasm, I still was eager to do the play. I had learned enough about the stage to distrust my own opinions. It did seem a worthy play, and Rice was a proven and worthy writer whose play I would have been happy to stage even had I thought it abominable. I also thought that excitement and even notoriety were healthy for the college drama. And finally Rice had promised to make himself available for the last week of rehearsals, and it would be, both for me and the students, a valuable experience to work with a man who thoroughly knew his craft.

I wrote Rice that I would like to do the play and questioned him about royalties and various other practical matters. His chief concern was the setting and the casting. He thought that the set need not be too realistic; it would be fine if it could merely suggest something of the majesty of Baalbek. About casting, a facet of production which he has always regarded as of first importance, he remarked:

> This is a quiet play, with little action. Its effectiveness will depend upon the solidity and authenticity with which the characters are projected. Do you plan to do it entirely with students? And if so, do you think they will be able to suggest the required maturity? When I did *Dream Girl* at the University of Michigan, I was able to corral some faculty members for the older parts, and that worked out very well. I really feel that this is of great importance.[1]

I wrote that I hoped to cast most of the major parts with older people, and he replied:

> What you say about casting is reassuring. I'd be a little worried about having some of the parts played by students.

As you know, it's much easier for young actors to suggest old age than to convey the solidity and maturity of the middle years. Of course, I don't look for topnotch professional performances, but I'd hope for some degree of verisimilitude.[2]

He also suggested that it would be helpful if I could visit him to talk the play over. I agreed, but I had not enough money to go to New York City, and it was only after several hours of pleading with deans, department chairmen, and boards of students that I managed to get an allowance for gas. The bill ultimately came to $10.61. Finances were a sore problem throughout the production. Although the play was a world première by a Pulitzer Prize winning playwright, I got only about $150 from the school, and the rest was raised by some of my students who sold about $400 worth of advertising for our programs.

When I saw Rice, I tried to get him to soften the character of Grue, the businessman, who seemed a stereotype of the Ugly American with a vengeance and so blackly black that I thought he would hurt the play. Rice disagreed and said that he considered Grue an accurate picture. He also added, with some relish, that he had called the character Grue because that was short for gruesome. I was somewhat disturbed by Rice's defense of what seemed to me purely a stage caricature.

The other character who bothered me was Davis, Suzanne's first husband. In the script, Rice seemed to describe him as having great potential value. Indeed, in one line that I omitted from performance, Suzanne remarked that Davis could have been anything he wanted—even President. Davis didn't seem to live up to the description, especially when he was contrasted, as the plot demanded, with the wise and civilized Dewing. It seemed to me that the plot would be stronger and Suzanne's choice more difficult if Rice made Davis more nearly Dewing's equal. Again, Rice disagreed. He thought it logical that Suzanne should be attracted to a charming man of her own age. A purely emotional attraction, he described it. He also surprised me by saying that the minor part of the Greek guide was a good comedy part and that even the walk-on of the Bedouin girl offered a good short part for some pretty young actress.

Our conversation emphasized our being at loggerheads over much of the characterization. It seemed to me that he conceived of his characters in terms of purely theatrical effect rather than of literary fullness. I thought that the danger of writing such characters was that you created only caricatures plausible for the moment on the stage, but easily forgotten afterwards. I even wondered if Rice, for all of his high seriousness, had not become harmed by the commercial theatre, perhaps even unknown to himself. At any rate, there obviously could be no major changes. The play was, Rice explained, something that he had spent a good deal of time on several years previously, but he thought that if he tinkered with it in any major way now he would only make it worse. He would, however, reread the play and attempt to cut it here and there, for he had always cut his plays in rehearsal.

In retrospect, I see that Rice was right in practically all of his opinions, and that mine were brashly inaccurate. At the moment, though, his opinions seemed depressingly wrong, but I thought that the university had probably gotten its $10.61 worth.

Sometime later, Rice mailed me several pages of revisions and said,

> Well, I got around to rereading *Love among the Ruins*, for the first time in years. At the risk of seeming to be immodest, I must admit that it didn't strike me as too bad. Anyhow, I think it deserves to be stood upon its feet at least once; and I'm eager to see what it looks like.
>
> I agree with you that the discussion in Scene Two is much too wordy and too static. Accordingly I have made substantial cuts and am enclosing the result. I think now the concentration of the contrasting points of view should help to keep the scene alive. Of course, what I wanted to emphasize is Davis' effort to impress Suzanne, which, as appears later, he succeeds in doing. As for Grue, I think he's just fine! I wouldn't want to change a syllable of him.[3]

Rice then left the country for about a month, and I began to block, cast, and rehearse the play. It slowly began to penetrate to me that if Rice had given in to my criticism of Grue and softened the character, he would also have fuzzed up Grue's allegorical or thematic value: Grue—business, Bicknell—the failure of the church, Dewing—the rationality of science, Davis—the fouled-up war generation that was just getting on its feet again. Consequently, I decided to play Dewing and Suzanne as full and thoroughly civilized people, but to play Grue as the script seemed to demand. Instead of playing down the Ugly American stereotype, I played it up for all it was worth. Rice had mentioned that I might cast the character against type, but I decided not to, thinking that this was merely a grudging admission and not what he really wanted. Grue, then, became a showier part than the others, and as rehearsals progressed it tended to get ever more broad.

To an extent, I decided to play the schoolteacher in this fashion also, and to eke as much grotesque pathos out of her as I could. I instructed the actress to develop a number of fussy, flighty mannerisms that I hoped would contrast nicely with the occasional deeply felt things that she said.

One character who bothered me was the minor part of Alma, the bishop's wife. She had little to do except listen to her husband and the schoolteacher, but she had two consecutive long scenes with each. I scanned the script minutely to find a possible hint of what the author wanted her to do, other than merely to toss in a sympathetic "Yes" or "No." There seemed some slight justification for her having helped to push her husband into church politics, and some of her lines might be read as disapproving of his disillusion and disenchantment. With this as a basis, I could play her as worried and abstracted during her scene with the schoolteacher, and as disapproving and finally conscience-stricken during her scene with her husband. This reading made the latter scene into a kind of argument and imparted a thread of conflict to it, rather than letting it be straight exposition by the bishop.

The bishop I thought a basically sincere and religious man who recognized his failure as both a churchman and a father, and who would be bitterly self-critical about it for the rest of his life. In my conception of both Alma and the bishop, I later learned that I diverged from Rice's ideas.

Rehearsals were in many ways disheartening. Unable to practice on the stage, we used what rooms were available. Often they were small and inadequate, and sometimes we could find no room at all. We rarely rehearsed in the same place two nights running. Rehearsals were also hampered by the bane of amateur theatricals—losing cast members and having people absent. Some absences were inevitable, but the loss of cast members is only inevitable in a school where dramatics are treated as an extracurricular social activity. Such a slapdash situation fosters a silly amateur egotism among the players, disturbs morale, and makes any kind of effective ensemble playing and growth almost an impossibility. In the course of rehearsals, my prompt girl and I played every part several times, and one of the characters I had to recast five different times.

With such rehearsals, the play appeared at first much less theatrical than I had originally thought, and much of the dialogue came out as awkward, overlong, and, in some of Davis' and Dewing's speeches about the creativeness of man, verging on the corny. Still, there finally came some improvement. When the main actors first came to the script, they thought the love scenes false and the language banal. I suggested, without complete conviction, that the language was truer and more dramatic than they thought, and that they were judging the realistic dramatist Rice by some inappropriate standard, such as the dialogue of Shakespeare or O'Casey, who had recently been done on campus. As rehearsals progressed, and the actors worked more into their parts, they began to see that Rice's lines had allowed them to probe their characters' emotions with great accuracy. The lines began to seem more appropriate and to chart, despite their simplicity, accurate and growing depths of feeling. They were discovering, and so was I, that realistic dialogue is a guide rather than a complete chart of emotion, as is Shakespeare's dialogue.

Despite these bright spots, the whole show in the next to last week before performance was still raggedly amateurish. To make matters worse, the stage was unavailable until the week of performance, for either rehearsals or constructing the set. Putting off the construction of the set until the last week was both unavoidable and terrifying, for we needed, among other things, a wall twenty-four feet long and eight feet high, upon which half a dozen people could walk and upon which we could mount four massive twelve-foot columns. In the amateur theatre, practically everything is done the hard way.

Rice appeared for the last week of rehearsals, and on a rainy Monday night he saw our first run-through on the bare stage. He thought that the three main parts were played quietly and solidly, but that Grue and Laura were much overplayed, the first being more a monster than a human being and the other more theatrical than real. His feelings about these roles posed me the most difficult problem of the week—other, of course, than the construction of the set—for I had to discard some of my own preconceptions. It finally came through to me, however, that toning these roles down was rather like the defense of the play's language that I had made to the actors. The character on the page was like the dialogue on the page; it stood not for completeness, but was merely a key. On paper, Rice could give only the outline of an accurately observed character. An outline shows up the faults more clearly than a completed drawing, and I had been emphasizing that outline rather than trying to fill it in. On paper, Rice's characters often seem to be bald collections of characteristics which lean more closely to the theatrical cliché than to life, but in performance Rice expects his actors to discover that fullness which he had room only to hint at. I suppose I realized something about the nature of the theatrical experience, something that I had long before mentally assented to, but never actually felt. The play on paper was not the play, and that truism had finally some real significance for me.

Discussing the play with me several months later, Rice mentioned that as a general rule he cast against type and cited a number of instances. The role of the boorish taxi driver of *Street Scene*, he gave to an actor with an especially amiable personality. The rule seems to hold most for the casting of minor parts whose character the author has not been able to fill out fully in the playscript, and the effect in production then suggests not the stereotype but the full human being. The major roles Rice, of course, writes in fairly fully. Indeed, his practice is to overwrite these parts as a help to the actors, and then to prune the parts in rehearsal.

In subsequent rehearsals, Rice made several cuts. In the Carl-Florence bit in scene 3, he took out some redundant talk. He also wanted the scene played more for comedy on the boy's part, for the scene came after two quite somber ones, and some liveliness was needed. This Florence-Carl scene was a lovely little one, which we managed to botch on one night of performance and to omit entirely on the other. Rice's notion for the scene was the basically amusing one of a woman trying to seduce a young man who is too naïve to understand at first her intention. The situation is a traditionally comic one, and it worked as well for Henry Fielding as it still does. Rice wanted more comedy from his scene, however, than we were unfortunately able to bring to it.

On other nights, Rice cut the Florence-Carl scene even more, and he also cut a great deal of dialogue from the last Davis-Suzanne scene, after she had turned him down. Rice explained that the audience, once it had found out that she was turning him down, would not want to listen to a lot of explanation. He also mentioned that another reason for overwriting the script was that it was in rehearsal easier to cut material than to write in needed scenes.

Some dialogue in the third scene between the bishop and Alma was pared away, and Rice also made me reblock this scene. I had had the two characters merely sitting and talking, just as in the immediately previous scene I had Alma and Laura sitting in the same place and talking. Rice explained that whenever possible he liked a character to "take" the stage. Certainly, by having the bishop nervously prowl about, we avoided some static monotony and pointed his agitation.

Three or four students and I had been working on the set after rehearsals till three or four in the morning, and by Thursday night the set was in tolerable shape for dress rehearsal. At least, one could see what the set might look like, should it ever be completed. Despite the play's really needing about a week's more rehearsal to smooth it out, the dress rehearsal went fairly smoothly. I scheduled only a run-through of a couple of scenes for the next afternoon. Rice had wanted to run the whole play, but I couldn't have assembled all of the actors, and I couldn't have spared the time from working on the set. As I was busy on the stage, he took some actors out into the foyer and ran the scenes for me.

After the rehearsal of the Bishop-Alma scene, the actors came to me and said that Rice had changed the interpretation, and wanted to know how to play it. I told them to play it his way. He had changed Alma from the strong-minded woman that I had made her into something much more retiring. He was right, in that there were few lines that I could base my reading on, but I thought that his view made the part thinner. Still, it seems to me that the key man in the theatre is the playwright, and when a matter of interpretation of character is at stake the playwright's opinion should be decisive.

To Bishop Bicknell, Rice gave a number of forceful gestures. He apparently conceived of the man as more forceful and outgoing than I had. I thought that this characterization was not indicated in the script, but certainly his reading again proved that I was playing for the stereotype and he for fullness.

At about six o'clock, the stage was in tolerable shape, and I went home for a much needed bath. When I returned, I saw that the house would be depressingly small. The school with its three campuses had a total of about 7,500 students; the town had a population of half a million; and the play had received excellent publicity—indeed, Rice first read about it in a copy of V*ariety* which he came across in India. Nevertheless, a scant 150 people appeared. I had expected a thin turnout and a desultory reception by the students, most of whom had never heard of Rice. But I was depressed and surprised by the playwright being almost totally ignored by the faculty. The other American writers to appear on campus that year, a handful of academic poets and a literary journalist who gave the commencement address, were all highly touted and feted. Rice, the most distinguished American writer of the lot, had paid his own way and given his services free, but except for one hastily arranged dinner he was left entirely to himself. It was all, I thought, depressingly symptomatic.

When the cast was made up and in costume, Rice and I wished them well and then wandered into the auditorium, he to sit in the deserted balcony and I to wander about taking fitful notes. The first act seemed better received than I had hoped, and the second act went fairly well except for some amateurish fluffiness of lines. The real botch-up was when Florence threw a line in her scene with Carl and then went completely blank. He managed to get her off the stage, but most of the scene and all of its comic effect were lost. Grue and Laura had toned down their parts effectively, and Suzanne was doing well, though hitting her lines harder than when we had practiced in small rooms. At the end, there were a couple of unenthusiastic curtain calls.

Rice was depressed by the audience, and I tried, without much success, to cheer him up. Expecting less than he had from either audience or actors, I thought things had not gone badly. I had long since decided that the only way to regard amateur dramatics was to expect failure, and then to rejoice on those rare occasions when it was less than total. Although the performance was rough in many places and the direction uncertain, the show had good things in it, and it was possible to see the value of the play itself. Many of the minor parts were, as is almost inevitable in the amateur theatre, weakly filled, but everyone did his best, and you can't ask for anything more heartening than that.

The second night was better, and there were perhaps two-hundred people in the house. Laura drew a good hand at the end of her scene with Mrs. Bicknell, and the Florence-Carl scene even drew a hand. There was a ghastly moment in the last scene during Davis' fight with the Arab, when the Arab nearly went through a flat, but the audience seemed sympathetically disposed, and the end of the play was not greatly hurt. The cast got one more curtain call than on the first night, and the applause sounded firmer and more enthusiastic. Rice was sorry that we had only a two night run when the play was just beginning to get on its feet.

After the show it was necessary to tear down the set and throw it away. I thought this the most depressing business of all, for we were able to save nothing. There was no place to store it. After about an hour and a half, the cast and crew dribbled away to my house for a party, and I and two others were left mopping the stage in the dead and silent auditorium.

Later in the evening, I chatted with Rice about the reviews that had appeared in the local papers. I thought they were crueler than was justified either by the play's merits or by the reviewers' capabilities. Also, as the reviewers apparently approved of new plays being presented, I could not see why they were so fiercely intent on driving our customers away. Rice thought the reviews rather typical, and remarked that one never reads a review for sense, but only to see how many people it will bring into the theatre. After he had left, it occurred to me that he was the third eminent dramatist I had succeeded in depressing in just six months. That surely was some sort of amateur record.

In the next week, I sent Rice his royalty check and some reviews from the campus paper, which were a bit more enthusiastic than the town ones. I also apologized for not having been a craftier director. He replied:

> You certainly have no reason for self-reproach. Taking into account the limitations of budget, time, talent and institutional support; you did an excellent job. A director should

not be burdened with such great handicaps. Frankly, had I known how great they were, I doubt that I would have said yes to the production. But somehow I got the idea that this was a part of an organized and continuing program, with good facilities and solid university backing. [I had mentioned the drama festival of the Fall, and it no doubt misled him. Indeed, some New York papers were also misled, for they rang up to inquire about the university's dramatic program.] What bothered me even more than the smallness of the audience was the complete apathy of the university administration, the almost pointed ignoring of the whole business.[4]

A conversation I had with one of the university deans who also taught modern drama courses seems appropriate here. He asked me if I had been satisfied with the production, and I replied that I had but that I had been depressed by the university taking no formal notice of the playwright.

"Rice is a rather cold and reserved man," he said.

I replied that I thought that a superficial view.

He glared at me for a moment and then snapped, "Well, to hell with him!" And stalked off.

Rice's letter went on to say:

However, I don't regret having had the play done. It gave me the chance I've always wanted to see what it looks like, and it was an instructive experience. I enjoyed the association with you and the students, and I welcomed the opportunity to see college dramatics at work. The result is, I'm afraid, a downward revision of my hopes for the university theatre as a partial corrective of the evils of Broadway. If play production is to be merely a marginal activity without status, adequate funds or strong support by the administration and the students, then I think serious professional playwrights will have to look elsewhere for a forum.

Of course, some colleges treat dramatics as a serious activity rather than as an extracurricular activity for those students not agile enough to make the athletic teams. A fair number of schools could have given Rice's play a creditable performance. On the other hand, the capable college theatres usually seem incapable of producing any play not given a recent Broadway seal of approval. Probably Rice was right, and the serious professional playwright would have to look elsewhere for a forum, but for the life of me I could not think where.

9   THE SAVED

FROM THIS REVIEW of Elmer Rice's career in the theatre, three points, I think, emerge.

First, the American theatre, whether commercial or amateur, is not a place where the art of the drama can flourish. A rare genius like O'Neill may survive in a commercial milieu with little damage to his growth as an artist, but the careers of other writers will suffer. Some, like Odets, will succumb to an even bigger commercialism than Broadway's and graduate to the films, to spend the rest of their lives trying to weld an uneasy alliance between two contradictory careers. Some, like the brilliant Edwin Justus Mayer, will go to California and never return. Some, like Saroyan, will be just too downright individual to last in the streamlined world of Broadway. Some, like Williams, will be hurt by an uncritical acclaim and imitate their own faults. And some few, like Rice, will plug on year after year, still dedicated, still writing what they want, still sometimes having a lucky hit, but more usually finding it harder and harder to get their plays produced.

The central fable of Rice's novel, *The Show Must Go On*, seems instructive here. That novel showed how by a lucky chain of circumstances a meritorious serious play appealing to a limited audience was produced and how, its audience not yet exhausted, that play was closed to make room for a vapid musical which inexplicably had hit the public fancy. That fable is more appropriate now than when it was written, for the serious play finds it at present harder and harder to be produced. From its current direction, one might predict that Broadway in the next few years will come no closer to seriousness than further imitations of imitations, further studies in eschatology, further variations of absurdity—or perhaps even a musical version of *Oedipus Rex*. With Bert Lahr.

The doyen of Broadway critics, Brooks Atkinson, would disagree with such an analysis. In his review of *Minority Report*, Atkinson posed this rhetorical question about Rice.

> Has Broadway been a place where he could exercise his intellect? With the same alert and courageous mind, could he have had a better career in the law? The theatre is the most cruel of professions because it turns savagely on its own people—destroys many of them—yet, with all its faults, the theatre has been a good home for Mr. Rice. Although he entered it as a clever technician, it gave him the opportunity to develop into a writer who can dramatize ideas.[1]

That strikes me as an uneasy apology, perhaps even suggesting in its remark about "the most cruel of professions" a smarting conscience. Furthermore, the statement is wrong. That Rice was able to dramatize ideas effectively at the beginning of his career is proven by *The Iron Cross* and *The House in Blind Alley*, the plays which Broadway would not produce.

Even more inaccurate is Mr. Atkinson's assertion that Broadway gave Rice an opportunity to develop as a writer. Except for the lucky fluke of *On Trial*, Rice owes little to Broadway. Actually, Broadway consistently blocked Rice's growth. Broadway turned down his early serious work. Broadway did not support *The Adding Machine*. No commercial producer could be found for *The Subway*. Every producer on Broadway refused *Street Scene*, until it was picked up by the almost forgotten and desperate William A. Brady. *The Left Bank, Counsellor-at-Law, Black Sheep, We, the People, Judgment Day,* and *Between Two Worlds* were financed by Rice himself, and if he had not staged some of these plays they would not have been staged. Rice's last plays were done by the Playwrights' Company which Rice himself formed with four other writers, and most of those plays would hardly have been done by ordinary commercial managements. In sum, Rice made his own place in the theatre, and he owes less to Broadway than Broadway owes to him. Rice's measure of success does not prove that Atkinson's Broadway is a fertile testing ground for art; it merely proves that Rice is a talented and indomitable man.

The amateur theatre in the United States is, with few exceptions, hopelessly imitative of Broadway. My own experience in it is that one must overcome a monumental mass of torpor, timidity, hesitancy, egotism, and red tape to stage anything that diverges from the conventional. When the amateur theatre is actually moved to attempt something fresh, that production is expected to be superbly professional. Sometimes, of course, the amateur theatre may rise to a kind of professionalism, but most usually it can not. When a valiant amateur attempt falls short of high excellence, that attempt is fiercely condemned as highbrow hubris, and the theatre slides back into its groove of easy imitation.

It is not my purpose to suggest some easy panacea for the ills of the theatre. I know of none. Theatre in the United States is not the least bit likely to be subsidized by the government. Private repertory companies are not the least bit likely to be more commercially successful than they ever have been. The economic situation of the commercial stage is likely to grow tighter, and the selection of its plays to grow narrower and to proceed in as robot-like cycles of popularity as does television programming. College theatres are not likely to become more daring than they are now, and community theatres may find even more of their audiences wooed away by the 21-inch screen.

With such a glum outlook, perhaps the strongest hope for the theatre lies in whatever individual attempts at excellence can be fostered anywhere—on Broadway, off Broadway, or way off Broadway. Such isolated endeavors are only a guerilla warfare, and unlikely to ignite a renaissance of the drama. Nevertheless, such attempts might act as a theatrical conscience. If some individuals continue to produce the new, the ignored and the unprofitable but excellent, if they do not kowtow to whatever is commercially safe or currently touted, if they continue the hunt to revive the best of the old and to ferret out the best of the new, then, I truly think, there will always be hope for the theatre in the United States.

ii

The second point is that the quality of dramatic criticism in the United States is exceptionally poor. Academic criticism is learned but ineffectual, and confines its discussion of current playwrights mainly to those most approved by the journalists. Journalistic criticism is ignorant, but influential, and the reviews of two men, Taubman of the *New York Times* and Kerr of the *Herald Tribune* can make or mar the fortunes of a play.

Probably the nature of journalism makes just discrimination difficult. The Broadway reviewer has an unfortunate time schedule. He must dash from the theatre to jot down whatever off-the-cuff impressions he can in the few minutes allotted him before his paper goes to press. It is scarcely surprising that such criticism is poor. Really, it is remarkable that it has any value at all.

Journalism is not always quite so rushed, but even when there is more time for thought, other journalistic necessities may hinder judgment. To take one notable example, the stories written for the influential *Time* magazine may be written at a less than breakneck pace, yet the reviews of this magazine are about as frivolous as those of the daily press. *Time* is a news magazine, and its subjects are those with the most dramatic or topical value. In discussing such subjects, *Time* rarely avoids some exaggeration, and this tendency is amplified by the necessities of its own exuberant style. Few people would deny the talent of Tennessee

Williams, but few would couple him, as did *Time*, in the same paragraph with Sophocles and Shakespeare.[2]

To take a more relevant example, one might note *Time*'s review of three theatrical autobiographies—one by Bernard Kops, one by Shelagh Delaney, and one by Rice.[3] The Kops-Delaney review was the lead article in the book section, and these two books were judged "fascinating documents." The Rice review immediately followed, and its tone was suggested by its title, "Monotony Report"—a half-pun typical of the magazine's jargon. In its passionate pursuit of wit, the magazine rarely hesitates to jettison taste, judgment, and accuracy, and all three qualities are notably missing from these reviews. The Kops and Delaney books were extravagantly praised for their faults and the Rice book contemptuously damned for its virtues. The reviewer seemed irritated that Rice did not mention by name his mistresses. He included the gratuitous sneer that the book seemed "to have been put together by a civil rights pamphleteer." As a final fillip he pounced upon one line in the book's nearly five hundred pages in which Rice remarked that he did not care for the works of Thomas Wolfe, and retorted hotly that Wolfe would not have liked Rice either. We have here, I think, a typical instance of the journalist's lack of discrimination and of his eagerness to sacrifice perspective for good copy.

Academic critics usually have a theoretical soundness that the journalists lack, but many academic judgments are beside the point and treat plays as literature or history rather than as plays. Like the journalists, the academics ignore vast areas of the modern drama. Such omissions may be necessary for the journalist who is limited by the plays he has to review, but only their own limitations prevent academics from talking about any modern dramatist.

A quick way to discover which playwrights academics discuss is to glance through the main academic quarterlies devoted to the modern drama—say, *The Tulane Drama Review* and *Modern Drama*. The Tulane magazine is a trifle more avant garde, and *Modern Drama* a bit more traditional in its choice of writers, but neither has so far printed anything about Rice. In its first twenty-two issues, *Modern Drama* printed twenty-seven articles about Shaw, twenty-three about Ibsen, sixteen about Strindberg, ten each about Williams and O'Casey, six about Synge, four about Miller, and three about Maxwell Anderson. However, it did print more than one article about Cocteau, Lorca, Camus, Lenormand, Ionesco, Beckett, and Brecht, and it has given space to a number of closet dramatists, such as Yeats (seven articles), Eliot and MacLeish (four articles each), D. H. Lawrence (two), Thomas Wolfe, Julian Green, Robert Frost, and Edith Wharton. To date, it has printed no articles about Rice, Barry, Sherwood, Behrman, Howard, Kingsley, Kelly, Green, Mayer, and their other contemporaries who may be said to have originated the American drama.

This pattern is repeated elsewhere. The largest coverage of articles about literary figures is the annual bibliography published by *PMLA*, the *Publications of the Modern Language Association*. In the bibliography for 1962, one may note that American critics wrote much more about American fiction and poetry than about American drama. There were seventy-four articles and books on Faulkner, forty articles and books on Hemingway, twenty-three articles and books on Scott Fitzgerald, eleven articles and two books on Salinger, eleven articles and a book on Katherine Anne Porter, and even seven articles on Wright Morris. Among the poets, there were sixteen articles and a book on Wallace Stevens, sixteen articles about Frost, and ten articles and a book about cummings. Among the playwrights, O'Neill fared well, although scarcely as well as Faulkner, Hemingway, and Fitzgerald. There were ten articles and three books about O'Neill, eight articles and half a book about Miller, five articles and half a book about Williams, and three articles about Wilder. Once again, nothing about Rice, Barry, Sherwood, Behrman, Howard, *et al*.

One other way to discover which dramatists the academics discuss is to note how frequently certain plays appear in the anthologies and textbooks which academics edit. The most recent listing is probably in an article by Professor James T. Nardin, printed in *College English* for April, 1963.[4] Professor Nardin lists the seventeen most recent drama anthologies, ten including some modern plays and the rest only modern plays. Out of the 271 plays anthologized, Shaw was represented 17 times, Ibsen 16, Chekhov 14, Strindberg 12, O'Neill and O'Casey 9, Miller 8, Williams 7, Brecht and Yeats 6 each, Saroyan and Ionesco 5, Wilder and Odets and Anderson 3, Inge 2, Hellman 1, and Rice, Barry, Sherwood, Behrman, Howard, etc., not at all.

This spot survey may suggest that academics write chiefly about three kinds of modern playwrights. The first kind one might call The Early Classic, and it would seem to include Ibsen, Chekhov, Strindberg, Shaw, O'Neill, and probably nowadays O'Casey. The second kind one might call The Newsworthy, and it would seem to include Williams, Miller, Albee, and the group of dramatists loosely classified together under the title of The Theatre of the Absurd. The third kind one might call The Closet Dramatist, and is well typified by Yeats whose plays are discussed as poems rather than as plays.

The first category merely pays homage to those writers already canonized; the second takes its lead from the journalist; the third is an occupational hazard of being a professor in the age of William Empson. Actually, the second and third categories sometimes overlap when complex and ambiguous playwrights, such as Beckett, Brecht, Ionesco, or Genêt, make a newsworthy stir. At their best, the academics can call attention to real, ignored merit here—Eric Bentley's long crusade for Brecht is a notable example. However, this crusading spirit works within a narrow framework of interest, and dozens of vital plays and arresting writers lie outside its pale.

Some of the best remarks about the theatre have not been written by critics, but by producers and directors. The writings of Stanislavsky have been notably influential, and there is much to be learned from the accounts of the

Berliner Ensemble or from directors like Tyrone Guthrie or Hilton Edwards. Yet even Stanislavsky is most useful for his instructions about the training of actors, and not of great help in formulating a theatrical criticism. His remarks, like those of other producers, are most often simple, casual, and offhand—insights arising from the problems of a particular production. These are pieces to build a critical approach with, rather than a formulated method.

There is no reason, of course, to criticize a director for refusing to do the critic's job; still, this split between the critic and the practical workers in the theatre is unhealthy. Until the distance is narrowed, it will not be criticism alone that will languish; it will be the whole art of the theatre. The central problem of dramatic criticism today is to bridge this gulf between the drama as theatre and the drama as either literature or history or news. The formulation of such a criticism is a staggeringly difficult task. One will be able to do it neither by academic patronizing nor journalistic quips. What is needed is a deep theoretical knowledge and wide practical experience. In the American theatre, probably Harold Clurman and Eric Bentley come closest to qualifying, but neither has so far addressed himself to a full formulation of a practical criticism for the theatre. Both have, I think, practiced such a criticism in specific reviews.

Despite this plea for a theatrical criticism, this book attempts no broad formulation, and is not even particularly adequate as specific criticism of specific plays. Partly the reason may be explained by a lack of sufficient theatrical experience, but partly the reason is an inability to answer certain enigmatic basic questions about the nature of that criticism. It is not enough to accept the axiom that the play must be criticized as theatre. One must realize that a theatrical criticism requires a new set of criteria, but sometimes a theatrical judgment seems more puzzling than revealing. For instance, if the telephone scene in *Dream Girl* is successful, one should be able to gauge the quality of its success. How would it compare with the contract scene in *The Way of the World*? How would it compare with a chase scene from *Charley's Aunt*? If one's yardstick were purely literary, the answer would be easy: Congreve's scene is superb, Brandon Thomas's trivial, and Rice's much closer to Thomas's than to Congreve's. If, however, one's yardstick is successful theatrical effect, then everything goes topsy-turvy, for the Thomas chase scenes are inevitably successful, while Congreve can only succeed with bravura performances. If the Thomas kind of scene is theatrically superior to the Congreve kind, the standards of the theatrical critic are totally different from those of the literary critic, and *Charley's Aunt* is a better play than *The Way of the World*. Although realizing that *Charley's Aunt* works better, I yet recoil from saying that it *is* better, and so find myself in an ambiguous and untenable position.

Problems like these are, to me at least, inexplicable, and the judgments of this book are hampered by that fact. That remark is not meant as a gambit to disarm criticism, but as an aid to appraisal.

iii

And that brings us to the final point: which of Rice's plays are of continuing vitality, and what is his position in the modern American drama? To answer the question, we should consider what plays of Rice are currently produced. Below is a list, which the author compiled for me, showing the productions of his plays in the five years from 1958 to 1963.

	Stock & Amateur	Foreign	Radio & TV (Mostly foreign)	Total
The Adding Machine	83	8	1	92
Dream Girl	44	5	10	59
Street Scene	10	8	1	19
Street Scene (musical)	16			16

	Stock & Amateur	Foreign	Radio & TV (Mostly foreign)	Total
Cue for Passion	9	1	1	11
Counsellor-at-Law	5	1	4	10
Judgment Day	1	8	1	10
The Grand Tour		2	8	10
Two on an Island	5		1	6
The Winner		1	5	6
The Home of the Free	5	1		6
Not for Children	5			5
The Passing of Chow-Chow	3		2	5
See Naples and Die		2		2
On Trial		1		1
Between Two Worlds		1		1
A Diadem of Snow	1			1
Love among the Ruins	1			1

This comes to 188 stock and amateur productions in the United States, 39 foreign productions, 34 radio and TV productions, and, adding one professional production of *Cue for Passion* in the United States, one finds a total of 262 productions in five years. At first glance, this seems a fair showing, particularly if one considers that some of these productions, like *Dream Girl* in Israel and *The Grand Tour* in Scandinavia, ran for months, and that four of these plays are about fifty years old. Of course, in five years there are innumerable theatrical productions in the world, and Rice's 262 productions represent a minute fraction of the whole. It is impossible to arrive at any accurate estimate of how Rice fared in comparison with other serious contemporary dramatists, but perhaps an inaccurate estimate might be suggestive. *Theatre Arts* used to present a fairly full listing each month of plays done in the United States, and in its lists for 1958, I found 58 U. S. productions for Williams, 38 for Shaw, 22 each for Miller and Anouilh, 15 for Inge, 11 for Anderson, 8 for Ionesco, 5 for Eliot, and 3 for Rice. A cursory glance at the lists for succeeding years up to 1963 suggests that this pattern is fairly constant, with minor fluctuations depending apparently on the news value of an author. A popular film version of a play seems to have some effect in keeping a dramatist produced in the amateur theatre, as does also a Broadway success. Shaw, Williams, O'Neill, and Inge have apparently profited by such publicized acclaim. Playwrights who have had no recent commercial success— such as the deceased Howard, Sherwood, and Anderson, the semi-retired Eliot, and, of course, Rice—seem to continue in a decline of popularity on the amateur stage.

Seen in this light, the list of Rice's productions appears less satisfactory. It might also be noted that the list includes only about half of his plays. It is no great loss that *Wake Up, Jonathan, Cock Robin*, and *Close Harmony* have not been revived, but the absence of a masterly play like *The Subway* is more disturbing. Neither *See Naples and Die* nor the excellent *Between Two Worlds* was produced in the United States, and these plays had a scant three productions between them, so they may be considered "lost" plays. *Love among the Ruins* was a resurrected play given an amateur production thirteen years after its composition. In sum, Rice's recent production record is no fair reflection of his merit, for at least two of the "lost" plays are among his best work. From this list, one may conclude that Rice is not a forgotten man of the drama, but that he is not as vividly or accurately remembered as he deserves to be.

Rice, incidentally, does not brood over the failures in his long career. In an earlier draft of this chapter, I made more forcefully than now the point that Rice had had some poor luck as a playwright. Immediately he denied the fact.

Even going along with the "luck" concept for a moment, it seems to me that the whole On Trial business was about as much luck as anybody could expect in a whole lifetime. So, as you point out, were the acceptance of *The Adding Machine* by the Theatre Guild and of *Street Scene* by Brady. True, there were other things that didn't work out so well. Still, on average, going along with the luck hypothesis, I think that the balance is in my favor.[5]

In one sense, Rice is right. The theatre has supported him comfortably for fifty years, and he has had a share of acclaim. Being a well-balanced man, he refuses the pleasures of self pity now that the applause is less.

> I've taken some beatings—but who hasn't?—and I've been pretty unhappy when some of the things for which I had high hopes took a nosedive. But in perspective, I've had a busy and lively professional life, with a good bit of recognition and substantial financial rewards, and without too much compromise or departure from what I wanted to do and how I wanted to do it. What more can anybody ask? [6]

Although admiring the point of view, I think one might ask for an accurate appraisal of one's career. Without arguing that this book is accurate, I should hope its judgments would suggest that Rice should be remembered for fifteen or twenty plays rather than for three or four.

I think that *Dream Girl* might be demoted from the first rank of Rice's plays, but that *The Adding Machine* and *Street Scene* should be joined by *The Subway, Counsellor-at-Law,* perhaps by *We, the People,* and certainly by the three diverse and brilliant plays of his 1934 season at the Belasco—*Judgment Day, Between Two Worlds,* and *Not for Children.* Of secondary importance, but still of high quality are, I think, plays like *Dream Girl, Two on an Island, The Grand Tour, The Winner, Cue for Passion,* and perhaps *Love among the Ruins.* Of lesser importance, I should think, are the plays which, although containing excellent portions, are by their intentions unimportant or in their technique faulty—plays like *On Trial, Cock Robin, The Left Bank, Black Sheep,* and the three plays about World War II—*American Landscape, Flight to the West,* and *A New Life.* Finally, there are the plays which are either poor or "lost." The poor plays would seem to include *Wake Up, Jonathan, Close Harmony,* and the early potboilers. Of the approximately twenty unpublished or unproduced scripts which Rice has sometimes referred to, some are demonstrably and some conceivably of high quality. Both *The Iron Cross* and *The House in Blind Alley* retain some vitality. *The Sidewalks of New York,* which was only published in part, and *Life is Real,* which was only published in German, both sound provocative. If the commercial theatre had been conducive to seriousness of subject and experimentation of technique, some of these "lost" plays might have made Rice loom even larger as a figure in the American drama.

Rice has produced a remarkable body of work—large, varied, experimental, and honest. It ranges from frivolous entertainment to intense seriousness, from irony to pathos, from photographic realism to stark stylization. The best of it truthfully documents almost fifty years of American life; it castigates the follies, it expresses the confusions; and it suggests the remedies for many of the ills which have beset free men of good will in the twentieth century. In a theatre whose most currently prominent voices are the negative ones of a Williams or an Albee, the affirmations of Rice may be unpopular, but they will also be valuable.

Having fallen elsewhere into the enthusiastic error of puffing my subject at the expense of other writers, I hesitate to place Rice among his contemporaries. He has some merits that O'Neill or Anderson or Williams lacks, and they have some excellences largely absent from his work. Unlike O'Neill, Rice seems often to try more for scope than for depth, but his most ambitious plays tend to be his best. His high comedy seems less deft than Sherwood's.[7] His recreation of everyday language is sometimes less vivid that Odets' or Williams'. His whimsy does not take flight as airily as Saroyan's or Wilder's. His language makes no attempt to be beautiful as does Anderson's—thank Heavens. His work falls short of the rich verve found in the two best plays of Mayer.

On the other hand, the endings of *Street Scene* and *The*

Subway are as grippingly tragic as almost anything in
O'Neill. George Simon, his counsellor-at-law, is as memorable a victim of the rat race as is Willy Loman, and he has
probably placed upon the stage a greater number of fresh
dramatic types than any of his contemporaries. Much of
the dialogue in *Two on an Island* is excellently racy, and
most of the dialogue in *Street Scene, Counsellor-at-Law,*
and *The Left Bank* hit his contemporaries as vividly as did
anything later in Odets' Bronx or Williams' New Orleans.
Some of the whimsy, the parody, and the satire in *Not for
Children* and even in *Dream Girl* can hardly be bettered.
As a consistently experimental playwright, he is rivalled in
our theatre only by O'Neill; as a master of every kind of
plot structure he probably stands alone. He has had his
failures, but he has done, at one time or another, almost
everything consummately. And it seems fitting to close
with the tribute that another master of the drama, Sean
O'Casey, paid to him.

> He is a very clever man of the theatre; I wish I had some of
> his gifts, but then the Theatre walks beside him, or he
> shoves it before him the way a girl does a perambulator.[8]

POSTSCRIPT, March 1965: I have just read Rice's newest
plays, *Slaves of the Lamp* and *Court of Last Resort*. The
first is a comedy with some lively fantasy in it, and the
second one of Rice's modern moralities. I have some
minor reservations about the comedy, but the drama
seems to me the finest and strongest that Rice has written
in the last twenty-five years. Both have been for some
time unsuccessfully making the rounds of producers.
What an immense waste. But also what an exciting opportunity for someone with enterprise and a theatre.

2—The Potboiler

1. Elmer Rice, "Apologia Pro Vita Sua, Per Elmer Rice," *New York Times*, December 25, 1938, Sec. 9, pp. 3 & 5.

2. Elmer Rice, *Minority Report: An Autobiography* (New York: Simon and Schuster, 1963), p. 94.

3. *Ibid.*, p. 95.

4. Elmer Rice, "—And on the Other," *New York Times*, September 23, 1934, Sec. 10, pp. 1–2.

5. Clayton Hamilton, "Building a Play Backward," in *The Theory of the Theatre* (New York: Henry Holt & Co., 1939), pp. 265–75. The essay first appeared in a review in *The Bookman* for October, 1914.

6. Quoted in *Minority Report*, p. 108.

7. *Minority Report*, p. 103.

8. Elmer Rice, "Preface," *One-Act Plays for Stage and Study, Fifth Series* (New York: Samuel French, 1929), pp. vii–ix.

9. *Minority Report*, p. 141.

10. Letter to Robert Hogan, May 20, 1963.

3—The Experimenter

1. *Minority Report*, p. 199.

2. *Ibid.*

3. *Ibid.*, p. 204.

4. Letter to Robert Hogan, September 7, 1963.

4—The Realist

1. Elmer Rice, *The Living Theatre* (New York: Harper & Brothers, 1959), p. 210.

2. *Ibid.*, pp. 209–10.

3. Letter to Robert Hogan, September 7, 1963.

4. "Apologia Pro Vita Sua."

5. *Ibid.*

6. *Ibid.*

5 – The Social Conscience

1. "Apologia Pro Vita Sua."
2. *Minority Report*, p. 335.
3. "Apologia Pro Vita Sua."
4. Elmer Rice, *Two Plays* (New York: Coward-McCann, Inc., 1935), p. xviii.
5. In *Minority Report* (p. 342), Rice wrote: "I am convinced now that I had long been unconsciously intending to call a halt to my writing and producing activities. In little more than five years I had written eight plays; all but *Not for Children* had been produced. Two plays written earlier had also had productions. Of the nine, I had directed eight, as well as three additional companies of *Street Scene* and one of *Counsellor-at-Law*. Six of the plays I had also produced, two of them in a theatre which I owned and operated. In the same period, I had written A *Voyage to Purilia* and two motion picture scripts, had made a lecture tour, five trips to Europe (two of them extensive), two to Hollywood, two to the Caribbean and one to Mexico. It was a pace that could hardly be maintained."
6. Elmer Rice, "Elmer Rice Says Farewell to Broadway," *New York Times*, November 11, 1934, Sec. 9, pp. 1 & 3.
7. Elmer Rice, "Theatre Alliance: A Cooperative Repertory Project," *Theatre Arts Monthly*, June, 1935, pp. 427–30.
8. Quoted in *Arena* by Hallie Flanagan (New York: Duell, Sloan & Pearce, 1940).
9. Elmer Rice, "The Federal Theatre Hereabouts," *New York Times*, January 5, 1936, Sec. 9, pp. 1 & 3.
10. "Politics Charged to the W.P.A. by Rice," *New York Times*, January 25, 1936, p. 7.
11. *Arena*, pp. 67 & 221.
12. *The Living Theatre*, p. 160.

6 – The Patriot

1. Elmer Rice, "Two Dollar Top Results," *New York Times*, December 3, 1939, Sec. 9, p. 5.
2. "Apologia Pro Vita Sua."
3. Letter to Robert Hogan, September 7, 1963.
4. *Minority Report*, p. 393.
5. *Ibid.*
6. *Ibid.*, p. 408.   7. *Ibid.*
8. Letter to Robert Hogan, September 7, 1963.

8 – The Lost

1. Letter to Robert Hogan, January 19, 1963.
2. Letter to Robert Hogan, January 28, 1963.
3. Letter to Robert Hogan, March 5, 1963.
4. Letter to Robert Hogan, May 20, 1963.

9 – The Saved

1. Brooks Atkinson, "Two at the Broadway Bazaar," *New York Times*, September 22, 1963, Sec. 7, pp. 32–33.
2. *Time*, March 9, 1962, pp. 53–60.
3. *Ibid.*, August 30, 1963, pp. 62–64.
4. James T. Nardin, "Recent Drama Anthologies," *College English*, April, 1963, pp. 577–83.
5. Letter to Robert Hogan, September 7, 1963.
6. Letter to Robert Hogan, September 26, 1963.
7. In an earlier draft of this book, I remarked that comedy appeared fairly rarely in Rice's plays, and he quite accurately remarked in a letter of August 20, 1963: "Here I must demur, for I rather fancy myself as a writer of comedy. *See Naples and Die, Dream Girl, Two on an Island* and *Not for Children* are comedy from beginning to end, and evoke continuous laughter when performed. My new play, *Slaves of the Lamp*, is all comedy too (but, of course, you haven't read that). At least half of *The Adding Machine* plays as comedy, and there are many comedy passages in *Street Scene, Counsellor-at-Law, The Left Bank, The Winner*, and *The Grand Tour*. Even that roaring melodrama, *Judgment Day*, has an effective and well-placed comedy scene. I could also mention *Cock Robin, The Lady Next Door* and *Wake Up, Jonathan*, in which I had a hand. Well, I don't want to be shirll about it, but it's a point of honor with me."
8. From a letter to Robert Hogan, September 26, 1963.

A CHRONOLOGICAL BIBLIOGRAPHY
OF RICE'S BOOKS AND PLAYS

On Trial, novelized by D. Torbett. New York: Grosset and Dunlap, 1915. Rice's work on this novelization of his play consisted in correcting Torbett's completed MS.

"The Home of the Free," in *The Morningside Plays.* New York: Frank Shay, 1917. This volume contained an Introduction by Barrett H. Clark and three other one-act plays: "Hattie," a drama by Elva De Pue; "One a Day," a fantasy by Caroline Briggs; "Markheim," a dramatization of Stevenson's story by Zellah Macdonald.

"A Diadem of Snow," in *The Liberator.* New York: Liberator Publishing Co., Inc., April, 1918, pp. 26–33. This play is more easily obtainable in *One-Act Plays for Stage and Study, Fifth Series.* New York: Samuel French, 1929.

On Trial, a Play in three acts. New York: Samuel French, 1919.

The Adding Machine. New York: Doubleday, Page & Co., 1923.

"The Passing of Chow-Chow," in *One-Act Plays for Stage and Study, Second Series.* New York: Samuel French, 1925.

Wake Up, Jonathan, with Hatcher Hughes. New York: Samuel French, 1928.

Cock Robin, with Philip Barry. New York: Samuel French, 1929.

Close Harmony, or *The Lady Next Door,* with Dorothy Parker. New York: Samuel French, 1929.

Street Scene. New York: Samuel French, 1929.

The Subway. New York: Samuel French, 1929.

See Naples and Die. New York: Samuel French, 1930.

A *Voyage to Purilia*. New York: Cosmopolitan Book Corp., 1930. This satiric novel first appeared as a serial in *New Yorker*; it ran from the issue of October 12, 1929, to that of December 21, 1929.

The Left Bank. New York: Samuel French, 1931.

Counsellor-at-Law. New York: Samuel French, 1931.

The House in Blind Alley. New York: Samuel French, 1932.

We, the People. New York: Coward-McCann, Inc., 1933.

"The Gay White Way," in *One-Act Plays for Stage and Study, Eighth Series*. New York: Samuel French, 1934. This one-act play without words also appeared in *The New Yorker* in 1928.

Judgment Day. New York: Coward-McCann, Inc., 1934.

Three Plays Without Words. New York: Samuel French, 1934.

Two Plays: Not for Children and Between Two Worlds. New York: Coward-McCann, Inc., 1935.

Imperial City (a novel). New York: Coward-McCann, Inc., 1937.

Black Sheep. New York: Dramatists' Play Service, Inc., 1938.

American Landscape. New York: Coward-McCann, Inc., 1939.

Two on an Island. New York: Coward-McCann, Inc., 1940.

Flight to the West. New York: Coward-McCann, Inc., 1941.

A New Life. New York: Coward-McCann, Inc., 1944.

Dream Girl. New York: Coward-McCann, Inc., 1946.

The Show Must Go On (a novel). New York: The Viking Press, 1949.

Seven Plays (including *On Trial, The Adding Machine, Street Scene, Counsellor-at-Law, Judgment Day, Two on an Island*, and *Dream Girl*). New York: The Viking Press, 1950.

The Grand Tour. New York: Dramatists' Play Service, 1952.

The Winner. New York: Dramatists' Play Service, 1954.

Cue for Passion. New York: Dramatists' Play Service, 1959.

The Living Theatre (essays). New York: Harper and Bros., 1959.

Minority Report: An Autobiography. New York: Simon and Schuster, 1963.

Love among the Ruins. New York: Dramatists' Play Service, 1963.

Life is Real was published only in Germany under the title

Wir in Amerika, Komödie in drei Akten, translated by Heinrich B. Kranz. Berlin: Chronos-Verlag, n.d. (*ca.* 1928).

There have also been foreign editions, translations, inclusions in anthologies, and reprints of the above works, but they are much too numerous to mention. Rice has written about a hundred uncollected articles; some of the more important may be found in the back issues of *The New York Times.*

Of the innumerable articles about Rice, I have found the following two the most perceptive and helpful:

Ralph L. Collins, "The Playwright and the Press: Elmer Rice and his Critics," *Theatre Annual: 1948–1949.* VII. New York: The Theatre Annual, 1949, 35–58. One of the very best critiques: a long and detailed examination of the reception of Rice's plays by the press, containing many persuasive evaluations of the plays.

Meyer Levin, "Elmer Rice," *Theatre Arts Monthly,* January, 1932, pp. 54–63. An excellent consideration of Rice's work up to *The Left Bank* and *Counsellor-at-Law.*

A critically negligible but delicious little satire in dialogue about the Playwrights' Company might also be mentioned — Wolcott Gibbs, "The Best Plays of 1945 (A Prophecy in One Act)," *New Yorker,* January 29, 1944, pp. 18–20. For instance: "Mr. Rice: . . . 'Now, my play ought to be pretty simple. Big cast, of course, and I figure there'll be ten or eleven sets — we may have a little trouble with Niagara Falls, by the way.' "

INDEX